The Shape of
Medieval History

The Shape of
Medieval History

STUDIES IN
MODES OF PERCEPTION

BY
WILLIAM J. BRANDT

NEW HAVEN AND LONDON
YALE UNIVERSITY PRESS

Published with assistance from The Mary
Cady Tew Memorial Fund

CB
351
B67

The eye's plain version is a thing apart,
The Vulgate of experience

Wallace Stevens

Dedicated
with love and admiration
to my parents
Walter John Brandt
and
Pearl Lillian Jeans Brandt

Acknowledgment

If I were required to specify an only begetter of this study, I would have to say that it was a medieval preacher encountered in the first years of my graduate study (I have long since lost the reference) who interrupted his sermon to invite his learned audience to solve the problem of why camels have four legs and flies six. He changed what had been merely a suspicion into an unalterable conviction, that the men of the Middle Ages were incomparably more remote from us than modern medievalists are ordinarily willing to allow. Although I still do not know the answer to his question, my attempt to understand the ways of thought that permitted it has been directly responsible for the present study.

But of course a book cannot have an only begetter. I have accumulated many debts in addition to my debt to the preacher. Some of these are personal, and perhaps do not belong in an acknowledgment. But at some point in this arduous enterprise the criteria of relevance ought to be relaxed. I have not heretofore had an opportunity to acknowledge my boundless indebtedness to Majl Ewing and Albert Hoxie, both of the University of California at Los Angeles. Although I have learned much from subsequent teachers, particularly Josephine Miles of the University of California at Berkeley and Sears Jayne, now at Queen's College, these men made learning possible in the first place by introducing me to my intellectual inheritance in a way that required me to take it seriously.

Among the many people who have been involved in the book itself, I can only single out those who have responded nobly to unreasonable demands. Leonard Nathan of the University of California at Berkeley has been involved in the book from the beginning. Its major conceptions have been hammered out in conversation with him, and he has read every passage in at least three drafts. His value to the book has not been diminished by his inveterate hatred of "this's" which have no concrete referent.

Arturo Fallico, Richard Tansey, and Herman Shapiro, all of San Jose State College, read the entire manuscript carefully, affectionately, and critically, and it is likely that every other page is indebted to one or another of them. My friend Paul Piehler of the University of California at Berkeley likewise read the whole manuscript and gave me the benefit of his profound knowledge of the Middle Ages when we were the merest acquaintances. I would also like to acknowledge the helpful suggestions of Morton Bloomfield, of Harvard University, and the invaluable assistance of Jean Guedenet, whose knowledge of Old French illuminated many dark corners of aristocratic thought for me. I must also acknowledge two grants-in-aid from San Jose State College and one from the University of California which have spared me much grueling labor.

Lastly it is a great pleasure to acknowledge the contributions, editorial and otherwise, of my wife, Mayflower. In her editing, she had much help from Jeffrey Dye and Richard Ferrie. But this has only been the smallest of her achievements. Before we were married, the then-director of my graduate studies, Willard Farnham, warned her of the peculiar disadvantages of being a scholar's wife. In the years since she has learned with grace to understand what he meant.

W.J.B.

San Jose, California
September 15, 1965

Contents

Introduction

The major objective of this study is to define the word "medieval" (particularly as it applies to England) in a more fundamental way than has heretofore been attempted. It is eccentric in that it proposes to arrive at such a definition primarily through a scrutiny of the chronicles of the period from 1100 to 1400, and this choice of source materials should be accounted for.

In the first place, one must examine the concept in question. "Medieval" is a word that can be applied meaningfully to many different kinds of artifacts—to poems, to cathedrals, and to medical texts. Ordinarily, it designates artifacts created within a certain period of time and in a particular geographical area. But it means more than that; it means that the object to which it is applied is somehow typical of the artifacts of that time and place. "Medieval" designates a character recognized in many objects sharing a common point of origin in space and time.

To put it another way, the periodicization characteristic of Western civilization (I do not know about others) is a *general* phenomenon; the changes marking one period off from another appear at about the same time in many different areas of human activity. It may be impossible to produce on demand a typical example of an eighteenth-century mind for instance (as one critic of intellectual history considers an a priori necessity for any discussion of such a mind[1]) but it is surely a fact that a great many products of a particular century—plays, philosophies, histories, gardens— bear the same sort of impress, proclaiming by their very natures, as it were, their common origins.

To isolate the mental habits which give rise to such perceived relatedness is a proper scholarly objective. It is, consequently, the object of this study to isolate and bring to awareness those char-

1. Kingsley Blake Price, "Ernst Cassirer and the Enlightenment," *Journal of the History of Ideas, 18* (1957), 101–12.

acteristics, found in many different kinds of artifacts, which we recognize as medieval.

There must of course be qualifications. The definition of "medieval" which follows is by no means comprehensive. It is an attempt to get at the essential character of the Middle Ages at the most fundamental level. Many of the characteristics which scholars have generally agreed to call medieval have their origin, in my opinion, in the modes of perception which I attempt to delineate. But other important medieval characteristics may have no direct relationship to this study at all. In other words, this is not the definitive study of the meaning of "medieval."

The second qualification concerns the kind of enterprise that intellectual history must be. A term like "medieval" cannot include everything relevant and exclude the irrelevant. It is a word, and as such it bears all of the ambiguities which Wittgenstein has shown to be characteristic of language. Although I know of no clear-cut exceptions to what I have written in the following study in documents of English origin written between 1100 and 1400, I would not be dismayed to discover them. This study might still be of great value as a generalization about dominant modes of thought in the period; such generalizations are not invalidated by scattered exceptions. And there are dozens, perhaps hundreds, of sixteenth-century documents which seem to me to fall within the definition I have proposed for the word medieval in the following study. It would be very odd if it were otherwise. The question to be asked concerning the Renaissance is, are there not documents in considerable quantity which do not meet this definition, which represent something new in the world?

Ideally, an enterprise such as this ought to be undertaken by a scholar thoroughly versed in all of the artifacts of the period. But there is no such person. Practically, one must choose a limited body of source materials which will, one hopes, manifest in a useful and abstractable way the fundamental modes of perception of the period under investigation.

The choice of materials is therefore a crucial consideration for the intellectual historian; the validity of his findings will in large measure depend upon it. Unfortunately, this choice must be based upon a priori considerations of the relationship between particular classes of artifacts (cathedrals or whatever) and the mind creating them. This kind of psychologizing very properly makes scholars nervous, but there is no alternative. If we do not answer certain questions consciously before we select our materials, we will answer them incidentally in the act of selection. For instance, an intellectual history based on the philosophies of a particular time assumes that philosophy bears some constant and fundamental relationship to its own time. It may or it may not; the intellectual historian is surely obliged to consider whether or not it does, and perhaps, if he chooses to use philosophical texts, he is obliged to justify his practice.

In short, to attempt to write intellectual history without any sort of theorizing beyond the bare presumption of periods in human history is a chimerical undertaking and can lead to conclusions that are flatly absurd. The best that one can do is to choose consciously, in full awareness of the hazards implicit in the choice.

Three considerations have led me to base this study on medieval chronicles. First, taken altogether, they constitute a substantial body of materials written by men who fall considerably short of genius. The intellectual historian cannot be concerned primarily with the work of great men whose relationship to their time we must suspect to be eccentric. It may be convenient to refer to the late fourteenth century as the "Age of Chaucer," for instance, but it is foolish to assume that Chaucer was somehow typical of the period. Conceivably he was, but the odds are very much against it, and the assumption can have no support until we have established some criterion of the "typical" by recourse to a body of materials written by less distinguished men. Medieval chronicles are both plentiful and unmarked by creative genius.

Second, medieval chronicles have little of the antiquarian about them. They were written for their own time without much concern for the past. In this respect they are preferable to medieval philosophical writings. Like all human activities, philosophy bears the impress of its time. It is an attempt to deal creatively with that intellectual heritage; even worse, it is at the same time ordinarily engaged in a dialogue with the past. How is the historian to sort out these elements—the contemporary assumptions, the intellectual inheritance, the dialogue with the past—without knowing what they are in the first place? How is one to know in advance, for instance, which positions of Locke originated in seventeenth-century ways of seeing reality and which were strategies to avoid problems that he saw in Aristotelianism? Medieval chronicles present no such difficulty.

The third advantage of chronicles is of supreme importance. As I have said before, the intellectual historian must psychologize, at least sufficiently to recognize the difficulties inherent in any study of the human mind. The human mind is not a perfectly programmed computer, in which every value and every judgment belong to the same order of importance. It is purposive and manipulative as well as affirmative, and at least a great many human minds are given to systematizing as well. All of these activities are capable of producing beliefs. A politician today must "believe" in motherhood and flags, and it is unkind to suppose such beliefs are always cynically entertained, even though their function is obvious. Beliefs designed to manipulate ourselves or other people —in God, country, free enterprise, or whatever—are too close and too painful to be illustrated. Furthermore, all of us who think have strategic beliefs which we cherish because they function to complete some intellectual system or because they support other beliefs. This variety of beliefs is a human characteristic, and as Lovejoy's *Great Chain of Being* handsomely illustrates, one belief may have different functions at different times.

However, the human mind is not a great bag of beliefs, ideas, and values, in which a belief in the great chain of being, for instance, jostles a belief in providence, with perfect equality prevailing between them. The beliefs that constitute an important part of human mental furniture necessarily exist in some sort of dynamic and hierarchic relationship to each other. Over and over men are confronted by situations in which flatly contrary beliefs or values are relevant, and they act in these situations, often with little real mental strain. When Samuel Johnson answered "no" to Boswell's question whether he believed in God as absolutely as he believed in the present location of a particular tavern, he touched upon a great human truth. We do not hold all of our beliefs in the same way, nor are they of the same degree of importance.

The ultimate aim of the intellectual historian, I suppose, is to map such a hierarchy of beliefs as they are ordered at a particular

time. The immediate objective, it seems to me, must be the delinea-
tion of the fundamental ideas and beliefs of a period, because
surely other beliefs are ordered in light of basic ones.

How can we know what beliefs are fundamental and what are
not, in any particular instance? Many scholars—Whitehead,
Lovejoy, and Cornford, to name a few—have asserted what seems
incontrovertible, that the basic and most important beliefs of an
individual or a period are those which are not even conscious;
an individual reveals himself most significantly when he believes
he is being most matter-of-fact.

The materials which make available to the scholar this level
of thought vary from period to period. For the Middle Ages,
chronicles constitute an ideal source. The chronicler, like every
other human being who has undertaken the task of telling what
happened, had to select and establish relationships. If we do not
immediately recognize this selective and ordering process in
medieval chronicles, it is because the basis of the chronicler's
selection and the kinds of relationships he saw in the human
world were very different from our own. Furthermore, the medieval chronicler, unlike the theologian or the romancer, was not
engaged in presenting some consciously held ideal about events
and the actors in those events. He was confronted with a very
concrete task: to organize and make meaningful for his readers
the brute stuff of experience as it appeared to him. In a sense, he
was the interpreter of somebody else's drama. The romancer and
the philosopher, on different levels, were concerned about the
way things should have happened, about some absolute and ideal
ordering of experience. The chronicler, on the other hand, proposed to make clear the way in which things actually did happen.
His class bias and his theological impulses, the major limitations
upon his objectivity, are so obvious that they constitute no hazard
for the modern historian.

In other words, just because the chronicler proposed to relate
nothing but the facts, and because he used only the most obvious
and readily discountable strategies, he becomes an ideal source
for the modern intellectual historian. We can safely assume that
the repetitive patterns we find in the chronicles were implicit in
experience for the chronicler and hence a fundamental constituent
of his mental equipment. Nor can it be seriously doubted that this

unwitting contribution of the chroniclers to their account of the world was at the same time a part of the normative mental equipment of their readers as well. Chronicles may not take us as far as we would like to go in our understanding of the Middle Ages, but what they offer to that understanding has a degree of certitude beyond that provided by any other kind of source material.

So much for the theoretical basis of this study. A word remains to be said about practical considerations. Medieval chronicles are readily divided into two classes having little relationship to each other: the great number of chronicles written in Latin and ordinarily written by monks, and the smaller body of chronicles written in Old French or Anglo-Norman by laymen or members of the secular clergy. (The number of Middle English chronicles is inconsiderable.) These obvious differences readily distinguish two classes of chronicles which, upon further scrutiny, also prove to be different in almost every other respect.

The modern historian has no choice but to acknowledge these differences and to recognize the two very different ways of looking at the world in the Middle Ages represented by the two classes of chronicles. The distinction will be found to hold good to a surprising degree.

Because of the significance of this difference, it is necessary to be careful of terminology. The two classes of chronicles are ordinarily designated as religious and secular. These terms are misleading. The Latin chronicles are religious only by association; their prefaces frequently profess pious aims, but the chronicles themselves are never engaged, so far as I have observed, in presenting a religious picture of the world. God operates intermittently in them, as an interruption in a world which has its own naturalistic modes of operation. The Old French chronicles do not begin to present a complete view of secular life in the Middle Ages; they are concerned with the activities of one class, the aristocracy. Hence I propose to call the two traditions clerical (a more neutral term than religious) and aristocratic (a more specific term than secular).

The perceptual characteristics of the clerical chronicles (which are perhaps the most important object of the study) need some further illustration. My first thought was to illustrate their omnipresence in medieval documents by reference to the encyclopedias of the period, and particularly to that of Vincent of Beauvais, which is clearly preeminent by reason of its completeness and modernity. This project proved to be impractical, not because what I wanted to show was not in Vincent's *Speculum,* but because Vincent was a compiler so careless as to be unintelligible upon occasion. But Vincent led me to a concentration upon medieval attitudes toward nature, and furthermore it was their importance in the *Speculum* that led me to concentrate upon Isidore of Seville, William of Conches, and Albert the Great. I trust the reader will not be too disturbed to find a book on English medieval chronicles open with a chapter analyzing the attitude toward nature of three men, none of them English. There is no doubt, however, that these men represented the attitude toward nature held by English clerks of the period. The possible English substitutes—the Venerable Bede, Alexander Neckham, and Roger Bacon or Robert Grosseteste—would have led to the same results, with less assurance of normality. They were not as influential in England as their Continental counterparts.

CHAPTER 1

The Medieval View of Nature

The medieval view of the physical world is generally studied as a crucial stage in the development of modern science by the historian of science who approaches medieval materials already knowing the destination. His interest and his bias is to perceive change in a specific direction. This is of course perfectly legitimate, but a different kind of question might be asked of the same materials. Instead of examining them for their relevance (or lack of revelance) to the unfolding truth about physical phenomena, we can examine them as manifestations of a frame of reference which is absolutely a priori to any particular experience with nature and which is a major part of the cultural inheritance of any period. In other words, one can examine these texts as expressions of a system of expectations about natural events. We can look for the concealed major premises which constitute "the view of the world of a particular epoch."[1]

The approach that one takes makes an immediate difference. While the historian of science finds change (because that is what he seeks), the student attempting to understand medieval physical theory as a system of expectations is struck by the great continuity in the material. It is no accident that Isidore of Seville, who died in 636, is frequently quoted alongside passages from Albertus Magnus (who died in 1280) in an encyclopedia like the *Speculum Naturale* of Vincent of Beauvais. Albertus was incomparably more sophisticated than Isidore, but he shared with him a basic view of the world. If we consider their respective worlds statically,

1. Alfred N. Whitehead, *Science and the Modern World,* Lowell Lectures, 1925 (New York, Mentor Books, 1962), p. vii.

as fixed systems, the relationship is manifest; Albert's universe, in its constellations as well as its elements, is a detailed elaboration, with notable corrections to be sure, of the universe of Isidore. But more important, the principles thought to underlie Albertus' world, viewed as a system of activity and change, were consistent with the Isidorean cosmic structure, even though the Spanish bishop was hardly aware that motion and change were integral characteristics of the physical universe. It can be of some profit, then, to begin an examination of the medieval view of nature by an examination of Isidore's views on that subject.

The Natural World of Isidore of Seville

Modern physical science can be seen as a continuum between two poles, the astronomical and the atomic, and the search for a unified field theory suggests that there is some problem in the relationship between the two. Medieval theories of nature can be approached in terms of the same two poles, perhaps best labeled the macrocosmic and the microcosmic, and there is at least an analogous problem of relationship.

We can deal with the static world of the Middle Ages, nature with its movement abstracted, very briefly. For its microcosmic aspect, Book 13 of the *Etymologies* provides the text upon which the elaborations of succeeding centuries were commentaries:[2]

> The Greeks call a certain first matter of things, formed in no way at all but capable of receiving all bodily forms, ὕλην: from this these visible elements are formed, and they took their name from this derivation. The Latins have named this ὕλην "matter," and therefore every unformed thing from which anything must be made is always called "matter" . . . And the Greeks called elements στοιχεῖα in that they come together with each other in a natural *ratione*[3] among

2. W. M. Lindsay, ed., *Isidori Hispalensis episcopi etymologiarum sive originum* (2 vols. Oxonii, Oxford University Press, 1911), Bk. 13, ch. iii, pp. 1–2.

3. It seems unwise to propose translations for certain key medieval terms. There is no modern equivalent for the term *ratio* (sometimes translated as "reason" or "order"), and hence I prefer to leave the concept in its medieval Latin and invite the reader to deduce its significance from its usage—which is what I would be doing if I attempted to translate it.

themselves, so that at one time it returns from fire to its beginning the earth, at another from earth to fire; and then that fire goes over into air, air is thickened into water and water is thickened into earth. And again earth is dissolved into water, water is rarefied into air, and air is thinned out into fire. Wherefore all elements are contained in all others, but each one of them has received its name from that which it has more fully.

As usual, Isidore implied rather than stated fundamental principles. But the principles are apparent: matter was the basic substance about which one could do little more than hypothesize its existence. This existence was, however, necessary, because the perceived materials of the universe, the four elements (fire, water, air, and earth), changed form continually; the medieval mind immediately recognized this habitual alteration as an impossibility without a more fundamental substratum to assure the permanence, God willing, of the universe. Also implicit in Isidore's specified changes is the recognition that such changes depended upon shared qualities. Fire could theoretically change into earth (although the Middle Ages was generally sceptical of this possibility) because it shared dryness with earth; it could change into air because it shared heat with it. Similarly, air could change into water, with which it shared wetness, and water could change into earth, with which it shared coldness. Hence the microcosmic world of the Middle Ages was a four-link chain of paired qualities. (In Isidore's peculiarly arranged volume, these fundamental qualities, however, were relegated to the book on medicine.[4])

As a consequence of this eternal change in microcosmic nature, the perceived materials, air, earth, fire, and water, were never found in a pure state. A part of each was always at that moment becoming something else. Since men perceived the elements as composite, there was something elusive and esoteric about the very notion of an element: elusive in that an element was never to be seen in its pure state; esoteric in that the idea of "pure state" excluded the idea of change and required a state of affairs impossible to imagine. This impermanence of fundamental materials was to be an important characteristic of medieval physical theory.

4. Lindsay, 4, ix, 4.

On the macrocosmic or cosmological level, Isidore again sketched the basic outlines of the medieval view of nature, although some confusion is apparent. According to his account, the earth, *terra,* "which in the singular number signifies the whole orb," is placed "in the middle region of the *mundus,* standing in equal intervals in the manner of a center from all parts of heaven."[5] *Mundus,* as he makes clear elsewhere,[6] is the whole universe. At the same time, the orb, which has been equated with the earth, is asserted to be "so called from rotundity, because it is as a wheel . . . And everywhere the ocean flowing around encompasses its borders in a circle."[7] But in another passage,[8] he speaks of a *sphaera caelo,* manifestly a globe, surrounding the seven planets and having the earth for its center. Even without the help of Macrobius,[9] subsequent generations were certain to discover that a wheel cannot be said to be the center of a sphere equidistant from it at every point. Isidore also speaks of the eastern region of this world as being its head, *quasi facies,* and the north as its hind part.[10] The persistence of this sort of descriptive confusion[11] makes one wonder if men in the Middle Ages really visualized the world as a sphere at all.

For the rest, Isidore duly, and dully, enumerated the major features of late classical cosmology. The scope of his discussion is indicated by his defense of astronomy which, according to Isidore, derived its value from the fact that:[12] "It defines what the universe is, what is heaven, what the site and course of the sphere, what the axis and poles of heaven, what are the zones of heaven, what the course of the sun and moon and stars, and so

5. Ibid., 14, i, 1.

6. Ibid., 13, i, 1.

7. Ibid., 14, ii, 1.

8. Ibid., 13, v, 2.

9. Macrobius, *Commentary on the Dream of Scipio,* 1, xiv ff., Eng. trans. W. H. Stahl, Records of Civilization (New York, Columbia University Press, 1952), 142 ff. Stahl, in his introduction, pp. 16–19, and his footnotes to the above passage, provides copious references to the writers who in turn provided Macrobius with his cosmology.

10. Isidore, *Etymologies,* 3, xxx, 1.

11. For instance, Vincent of Beauvais retains without comment Isidore's entrance and exit for the sun (see below). *Speculum naturale,* Bk. 2, ch. i; *Speculum quadruplex* (4 vols. Duaci, 1624), *1,* col. 79.

12. Isidore, *Etymologies,* 3, xxviii, 1.

forth." The "and so forth" included hinges for the heavenly sphere to pivot on in its revolution around the poles[13] and, rather oddly,[14] two doors, one east and one west, for the sun to go through on its diurnal course.

The lack of interest which Isidore manifested in cosmology is surely connected with his out-of-hand dismissal of the claims of astrology. The profound interest of the later Middle Ages in the courses of the heavenly bodies was clearly due to the almost universal assumption that the behavior of these bodies was of immense significance to human life.[15] But Isidore was also able to dismiss the claims of astrology casually because he had so little concern for movement and change. The world that emerges from his pages is as nearly static as this variegated orb, tumbling through darkness, could be.

The reason for this peculiar stasis is that where we see change, Isidore saw successive and discontinuous states of being. This view of change is apparent even in the matter of the seasons.

> The times of the year are four: spring, summer, autumn, and winter. And they are called times from a mixing of shared things, since they moderate each other with moisture, dryness, heat, and cold. And they are called periods of time (*curricula*) because they do not stand but run. For it happened after the world was made that times were divided into three-month periods. Of which times the ancients make a distinction (*faciunt discretionem*) so that in the first month spring is called new; in the second, grown-up, in the third, descending . . . (and so with the rest). Spring is so called because it is verdant. For then after winter, the earth is dressed in herbs, and all things burst into flower. Summer is so called from flaring heat (*aestu*), that is, from heat, and flaring heat as if burnt up (*usta*), that is, burnt up (*exusta*) and dry. For heat is dry. Autumn is so called from season [or stormy weather] (*tempestate*), when the foliage of trees falls and all

13. Ibid., xxxvii, 1.
14. Ibid., xl, 1.
15. As Professor Thorndike has put beyond doubt. See especially *The History of Magic and Experimental Science* (8 vols. New York, Columbia University Press, 1923–58), 2, 253–54. Isidore's out-of-hand dismissal of the claims of astrology is found in the *Etymologies,* 3, xxvii.

things mature. The *ratio* of the hemisphere has been called winter, because then the sun revolves in a briefer circle.[16]

The distinctness of the seasons is the notable thing about this passage. These three-month periods are not descriptive of succeeding climatic or meteorological states that have any relationship to each other (although elsewhere he makes each dependent upon the position of the sun);[17] they are real entities in the nature of things. The self-subsistent character of the seasons stands out the more sharply in comparison with their monthly divisions. The "ancients" divided the seasons; although the distinctions seem rather sharply drawn, they were of human origin and presumably for human convenience. The seasons, on the other hand, represent successive states of being (if that is the right word) of a very peculiar kind.

For Isidore time itself was divisible into a succession of ultimate and irreducible particles. In his discussion of atoms (derived from Lucretius), he asserted that there were atoms "in a body, in time, and in number."[18] There must be, he argued, a thing which is finally indivisible, in a year as well as in a stone. Both indivisible entities were analogous to the number "one."[19]

> A moment is the least and most limited time, so called from the movement of the stars. For it is the extremity of an hour in brief intervals, when anything changes and succeeds itself. Hour is a Greek name and nevertheless it sounds like Latin. For the hour is the end of time, just as mouths are the end of a sea, of rivers, and of garments (*vestimentorum,* which might be translated "skins").

A week apparently had the same kind of semiphysical status; the sun was the chief of all stars, "just as the same day [Sunday] is the head of all the days together" (*cunctorum dierum*).[20]

Isidore's comparison of time, water, and garments (of all things) indicates that it was not merely divisions of time that acquired the status of separate entities; the mouth of a river had the same

16. Isidore, *Etymologies,* 5, xxxv, 1–6.
17. Ibid., 30, li, 2.
18. Ibid., 13, ii, 2.
19. Ibid., 5, xxix, 1–2.
20. Ibid., 13, xxx, 5.

sort of independent status and reality. This attitude applied to words as well; an object, a self-subsistent entity, loomed behind almost every noun that came into Isidore's purview.[21]

Isidore's world was astonishingly static; the lack of movement and change in this world can hardly be exaggerated. Some movement there was, but it did nothing to blur the splendid isolation of its self-subsistent entities because it was never really a relationship between objects; it was habitually located within a particular object. Movement and change were self-generated, and the entity itself was a sufficient principle for the explanation of its subsequent states and activities. Hence variegated and various appearances might be explained by mere reference to the nature of the objects in the world.

This approach to physical phenomena is seen most clearly, perhaps, in the long enumeration of animals in Book 12. A single example will suffice for illustration. Isidore says of goats:[22]

> The male goat is a wanton animal, apt to butt and burning always to coitus, whose eyes look cross-eyed on account of lust. Whence he has drawn his name. For according to Suetonius (Prat. 171), he-goats are squint-eyed. Whose nature is so hot, that adamant, which the matter neither of fire nor of iron is strong enough to break, is dissolved by the blood of the he-goat. The large he-goats are called *Cinyphii* from the river Cinyps in Libya, where large ones are born. Some are called *capros* and *capras* from plucking thickets. There are others that tear at rough things. Some, from the creaking of their shanks, are called *crepas;* there are wild she-goats, which the Greeks have named δορκάς in that they see most acutely, that is ὀξυδερκέστερον. For they are accustomed to dwell in the highest mountains, and they see all who come, however far off they may be.

21. The rare exceptions to this generalization are better evidence for its truth than the infinite number of passages that might be quoted in its support. For instance, Isidore felt obliged to explain to his readers that darkness and silence were not things, but the absence of light and sound respectively. The tone of the passage makes it evident that Isidore was dealing with a conception esoteric to himself as it was to the reader. Ibid., x, 1.

22. Ibid., 12, i, 14–15.

Characteristic ways of behaving are attributes; they are part of the fundamental definition of the object. Squint-eyes and butting, for instance, are not differentiated; their status in relation to goats was of absolutely the same order.

It was at least theoretically possible, according to this view, to exhaustively describe a goat, to arrive at the essence of goatness, so to speak, by such a list of attributes, specified without relationship to anything else in the universe. This characteristic of Isidorean thought is characteristic of medieval thought generally. More will be said later; here it is sufficient to note that such an approach to the phenomenal world prohibits explanation and, in any modern sense, understanding. The questions that concerned men in later times could not be asked by Isidore.

For instance he tells us,[23] in the same section on goats, that wethers have worms in the top of their heads which make them butt each other. Here is a double relationship: wethers have worms, and worms make them butt. But if the reason for the worms should be sought, the answer could only be, "Wethers have such worms." Worms were a part of wether nature, and hence butting was an aspect of wether nature, once removed. Likewise the livers of mice wax, Isidore tells us,[24] with the waxing of the moon, just as certain maritime animals swell up. But the connection between the livers of mice and the moon was obscure. Indeed, Isidore did not, and could not, ask the question about such connections. A relationship was inherent in the nature of mice livers, and waxing was the inevitable consequence.

This action–object relationship is even more striking when no object is immediately at hand to account for a particular action. Here is Isidore's explanation of thunder:[25]

> Thunder is so called because its sounds may terrify, for tone is sound. Which therefore at times shakes all things so violently that it seems that heaven has been rent, when a hurricane of most violent wind launches itself suddenly at clouds, and with an increasing eddy seeking an exit it rips up the cloud, which it has hollowed out, with a great blow,

23. Ibid., i, 10.
24. Ibid., iii, 1.
25. Ibid., 13, viii, 1–2.

maintaining if only to keep the scientific contributions of the Platonic revival from being lost entirely, since this contribution is substantially represented by at most a half-dozen writers—Thierry of Chartres, Honorius Solitarius, Gilbert of Poree, Bernard Sylvester, perhaps Adelard of Bath, and most important of all, William of Conches, who is the chief subject in the following analysis.[30] One might also include Alexander Neckham, whose scientific attitudes are twelfth-century even if his use of Aristotle is thirteenth-century. One can safely neglect that much-studied anomaly of this period, Hildegard of Bingen, because physical nature was, for her, merely an adjunct of prophecy.

One advantage of paying due attention to these twelfth-century writers on cosmological theory is that they enable us to judge better the significance of Aristotle to the Latin West. We will observe in the first place that medieval cosmology received its definitive formulation before the Aristotelian revival. Except for the introduction of the notion of a fifth and ethereal element, Aristotle left medieval cosmology, statically viewed, as it was, and the fifth element proposed a distinction without a great difference, since the twelfth-century scientists had already concluded that the heavenly fire was quite unlike earthly fire and hence as mysterious as any fifth element.[31] Otherwise Aristotle was commentary and elaboration upon a cosmology already well understood. This relationship is clearly seen in the encyclopedia of Vincent of Beauvais, in which it was standard practice to set up a lengthy quotation from William of Conches (very likely because he excelled in succinctness) for topics requiring cosmological description and to supplement this description by passages from

30. For a text I have used the *De philosophia mundi libri quatuor* ound in the *Opera* of Honorius Augustodunensis (*Patrologiae cursus* mpletus, Series Latina, ed. J. P. Migne [221 vols. Paris, 1844–64], after referred to as *MP*), *MP*, 172, cols. 39–102. At times it has been sary to correct this text by that found among the works of Bede, o, cols. 1127–78. Both texts seem to have been reprinted verbatim ixteenth-century editions, and neither inspires much confidence. tly Vincent of Beauvais seems to be quoting from a better and t than either of these. I was not able to make use of a sixteenth- dition, *Philosophicarum et astronomicarum institutionum* irsaugiensis olim abbatis libri tres* (Basilea, 1531). am of Conches, *De philosophia mundi*, Bk. 3, sec. 2; *MP*,

and thus it is borne to the ears with a terrifying crash. About which one ought not be amazed, since a little bladder burst also emits a great sound.[26] And lightning is squeezed out at the same time as thunder; but that is seen more quickly, because it is clear, and the former seems to reach the ears more slowly.

The science of Isidore's day did not have the techniques and the instruments even to approximate the modern approach to meteorology; we do not pause at the absurdity of the explanation. But notice that Isidore, confronted with the inexplicable physical event, posited a unique object, a hollowed-out cloud, which, from its own inherent nature, gave rise to a unique event, thunder. The same impulse to posit a unique object with unique—and hence inexplicable—qualities is apparent in Isidore's remark on lightning. The peculiar clearness of lightning was equally inexplicable.

Consequently the events that comprised the physical universe always tended to be changes from one unique status to another. In effect, a change was the alteration of one unique object into another unique object. For instance, Isidore says of the air in the lower part of this enclosed sphere:[27]

For greatly moved it makes winds; moved more rapidly, fires and thunders; contracted, clouds; thickened, rains; in congealed clouds, snow; in more forcefully congealed and denser clouds, hail; distended, it brings forth clear weather. For air made dense is a cloud; a cloud rarefied and dissolved is air . . . And the winds gather together the air and make a cloud.

It is a mistake to see a succession of potential or actual states of a natural object here; what we have is rather a succession of objects. The changes are transformations, and the actions which brought about these changes were unique and unaccountable—a faculty

26. This habit of reasoning by analogy from the common and observable to the uncommon and unobservable goes back, of course, to early classical times. See that small jewel of a book by F. M. Cornford, *The Laws of Motion in Ancient Thought* (Cambridge, England, Cambridge University Press, 1931).

27. Isidore, *Etymologies,* 13, vii, 1–2.

of the substances themselves. As there was no principle of continuity between one state and another, so there could be no principle of movement governing such changes. Both the changes and their results were self-subsistent, even though they inhered in objects, and the results were self-subsistent and unique.

This, then, was the Isidorean inheritance, and Isidore was without peer as a medieval writer on physical nature and physical theory until the twelfth century,[28] and as we have seen, Isidore was never really rejected by the writers of the twelfth and thirteenth centuries. In view of his continued relevance to later thought, it will perhaps be useful to summarize the two principles of the *Etymologies* which medieval scientists were to see as principles implicit in the workings of the universe.

In the first place, Isidore regarded the natural objects of this world as self-subsistent and self-explanatory (insofar as explanation was possible from the Isidorean point of view), and this status was habitually extended to concepts that we would not regard as natural objects—the mouths of rivers, for instance. The fact that all of these objects presumably originated in the will of God was irrelevant to Isidore's perception; God did not, obviously, function as an explanatory principle; to say that God is the origin of all things is not to propose a perceivable relationship among them.

The structure of the *Etymologies* itself testifies to the discreteness of objects; there is no rational principle at work in the large-scale organization of its twenty books. The mass of secondhand fact that Isidore had accumulated could only be presented in terms of some arbitrary schemata. The basic point of view prohibited any meaningful organization.

There is little doubt that the later Middle Ages, in its struggles for unity and order, sought a coherent universe. But there can be little doubt, also, that the Isidorean presuppositions were too

strong. The universe remained one of discrete and minimally related objects throughout the period.

The second surviving Isidorean conception was his notion of the nature of motion and change. Motion was an inherent capacity, or necessity, of a particular object. Change was one object working upon another object and inducing an alteration of substance—inducing a transformation into another object, in effect. A new object, or a new substance, emerged (Isidore would have been troubled by the distinction). But change was neither the result of interaction nor relative. This fact, too, had its consequences for subsequent thought. The scientists of the later Middle Ages increasingly saw motion and change as constituting their preeminent problem. But at least to the time of Albert the Great (the terminus of this survey), motion and change were thought of as latent characteristics of specific objects, or as one-dimensional relationships between two objects.

The physical theory of the later Middle Ages bore little superficial resemblance to Isidore's primitive descriptions. The introduction of the physical theorizing of Plato, by means of the *Timaeus* and certain Neoplatonic sources, permitted the twelfth century to impose a kind of order on the jumble of the *Etymologies,* and these sources gave point and direction to further theorizing. The impact of Aristotle upon the thirteenth century was, of course, overwhelming. Yet these later developments merely expanded and subtilized the understanding of nature implicit in the works of Isidore of Seville; they did not overthrow it. The Isidorean inheritance did not become irrelevant to the Middle Ages.

William of Conches and the Science of the

There were two distinct intellectual movements in the twelfth century. The first was the Platonic movement associated with the School of Chartres; this was largely conservative and static in intention and inspiration. The second was the great scientific revival, culminating in the recovery of almost all of Aristotle. And the two were frequently confounded, as by the

---

28. This is particularly apparent in the great thirteenth-century encyclopedias of Vincent and Bartholomew in which one finds a hundred citations of Isidore for every citation of Cassiodorus or Bede. Pliny apparently survives in more manuscripts from the early Middle Ages (see A. C. Crombie, *Medieval and Early Modern Science* [2 vols. New York, Anchor Books, 1959], *I*, 11), but in the later encyclopedias Pliny does not rival Isidore in importance. It is my impression that Isidore is far more important in other kinds of scientific writings as well.

29. C. H. Haskins, *The Renais*... York, Meridian Books, 1957), pp. 3...

more recently accepted authorities, including Albertus Magnus and Aristotle.

It is in the twelfth century, and not the thirteenth that one first sees the medieval search for some embracing system to give intelligibility to the whole universe; the twelfth century, moreover, raised the ideas of movement and change to problems of the first magnitude. The reception of Aristotle was due in no small degree to the facts that he seemed to offer a solution to problems which had already been recognized and that the terms of his solution were appropriate to the earlier formulation of that question. At the same time, of course, the twelfth century was the bridge between Isidore and Albertus Magnus, a bridge which makes the continuity of medieval thought unmistakable.

The superiority of twelfth-century cosmology over the cosmology of Isidore lay in the clarity of its arrangement. William of Conches, making liberal use of the *Timaeus* and Constantine the African,[32] clearly visualized the circle of the fixed stars, an area of planetary circles (about which he was not so clear[33]), and the four elements layered underneath;[34] he offered the image of an egg, with the elements corresponding to albumen, yolk, and so forth.[35] This comparison was apparently a common way of visualizing the universe in the twelfth century.[36] His discussion of the fixed stars and the seven planets was thoroughly respectable. While the elements of William's cosmology were generally known to Isidore, they emerged as a system in the *De philosophia mundi*.

With the help of these same two sources, the *Timaeus* and Constantine, William was able to explicate the elemental nature of the world with great fullness. William defined an element as something simple in quality and least in quantity; it achieved a status, as Duhem points out,[37] that it had not attained for previous medieval writers on the subject. William argued at length that

32. For a discussion of William's sources see Pierre Duhem, *Le Système du monde* (10 vols. Paris, Hermann, 1913–59), *3,* 87 ff.

33. William of Conches, *De philosophia mundi*, 2, vi–xvi; *MP, 172,* cols. 59–62.

34. Ibid., 1, xxi; *MP, 172,* cols. 52–56.

35. Ibid., 4, i; *MP, 172,* col. 85.

36. Vincent of Beauvais quoted Comestor to this effect (*Speculum naturale*, 3, i; col. 161), and the analogy appears also in an apparently genuine work of Honorius, *De imagine mundi*, 1, i; *MP, 172,* col. 121.

37. Duhem, *Le Système, 3,* 103.

an element was a conjunction of qualities and not merely a mixture, and he explicated competently the Platonic notion that air and water were necessary to join the more basic elements of fire and earth.[38] Each element was to be found through the universe (he argued that the stars must be coagulated earth and water[39]), but the zones of the universe took their names from the element that predominated in each one.[40] William was very much aware of the qualities which composed the elements, hot and cold, wet and dry; they became, in medieval thought, more significant than the elements themselves, because such qualities defined the level of manipulation. Herbal medicine, for instance, was primarily related to the scientific view of the universe through the ascription of these qualities to herbs.[41] But these are changes in detail and emphasis; the universe, statically viewed, was essentially the same for both William and Isidore.

Both the macrocosmic and the microcosmic accounts of the universe provided principles of motion by which specific events might be explained. The macrocosmic account suggested, quite obviously, an essentially astrological (or at least astronomical) explanation of events. The microcosmic account implied an explanation which depended upon the medieval (and classical) equivalent of gravitation.[42] These were alternative possibilities throughout the Middle Ages. Macrobius, for example, was an explicit source for the astrological explanation,[43] and Isidore's account might be called gravitational. Each system depended upon the other. But the twelfth century sought principles of motion and change in the microcosm. William of Conches was basically committed to the gravitational view because his was a self-

38. William of Conches, De philosophia mundi, 1, xxi; MP, 172, cols. 51–52. The attention that William devotes to proving the existence and ultimate nature of an element suggests that this was a conceptual problem in the twelfth century.

39. Ibid., col. 54.

40. Ibid., col. 49.

41. Or, at least, it was by attention to such qualities that medieval herbalists hoped to generalize their art beyond the merely empirical. Brief scrutiny of The Herbal of Rufinus, L. Thorndike, ed. (Chicago, University of Chicago Press, 1946), will show how often individual herbs were classified according to their elementary qualities.

42. See below, p. 15, for the account of medieval "gravitation."

43. See particularly Dream of Scipio, 1, xv–xx; pp. 148–74.

subsistent universe. The ultimate principle of motion that Aristotle and the thirteenth century were to ascribe to a *primum mobile* William attributed to fire which, being frustrated by the spheres of the planets and fixed stars in its natural impulse to move eternally upward, developed a circular motion, carring the very spheres of heaven around the earth.[44] Thus even astrological phenomena, to which William ascribed considerable influence,[45] had an essentially gravitational basis.

This behavior of fire was somewhat eccentric in William's general scheme. His ordinary assumption about the physical world of the four elements was that each element had its natural place in a closed and finite cosmos. The basic elements were fire at the outermost limits of this cosmos and earth at its center, with their relative weights determining their positions. But this was not really a gravitational system; it is generally described by twentieth-century scholarship as a system of dynamic equilibrium (which is perhaps to flatter it). There was a proper place for each element in the scheme of things. Fire did not merely have less weight than earth; it had lightness. Air had less lightness and sought the place of less lightness below fire.[46] But movement could nevertheless be explained, in this medieval counterpart of gravitational theory, as due to a displaced element seeking its proper place in the universe. The same sort of movement could of course be explained by the attraction of the same for the same; fire rose because it was attracted by heavenly fire.[47] These explanations came essentially to the same thing.

But this "gravitational" principle was limited. It explained why fire went up and rocks went down, but if fire and rocks were allowed to behave in this obvious fashion for very long, without the operation of some other principle, the world would have shortly presented the neat stratification of a layer cake. However dear immobility (as an ideal, at least) may have been to the medieval heart, this arrangement was obviously an inadequate

44. William of Conches, *De philosophia mundi,* 2, xvi; *MP, 172,* cols. 61–62. The structure of the *De philosophia* shows the same thing; William begins his discussion of the universe by a discussion of the elements and how they behave.

45. Ibid., 2, xvii ff.; *MP, 172,* cols. 62 ff.

46. Ibid., 1, xxi; *MP, 172,* col. 53.

47. See below, p. 18.

description of the world. And yet the twelfth-century scientist was only occasionally aware of the difficulty. The *De imagine mundi,* by Honorius Solitarius, suggested that these elements revolved "in the manner of a circle," with earth passing into water, water into air, air into fire, and fire back into earth.[48] But this solution was stillborn. Fire obviously did not pass back into earth in any great quantity,[49] even though it shared a quality (dryness), with earth. Neither Honorius nor any later thinker, so far as I have observed, made an attempt to exploit this circularity in the development of a cosmology. The problem was generally ignored in the twelfth century.

It never presented itself very forcefully because twelfth-century thinkers shared with Isidore a way of perceiving spontaneous generation of action and change as a part of the very nature of objects. This manifested itself at times as a kind of naïve analogizing. Such was Adelard of Bath's explanation of thunder. Everyone has observed, he pointed out, that moist fumes arise, and likewise everyone knows that the winds in the upper atmosphere are cold. Obviously cold winds freeze moist fumes, making a large sheet of ice, which was "kept firm by its own extent and cohesion and supported unbroken by the air beneath it." But headwinds may swoop down and break it, or it may be weakened and finally broken by the heat of the sun. The large bang of the breaking ice was, clearly, thunder. As Adelard confidently asserted: "Nothing is difficult unless one loses heart."[50]

Such explanations are common. William of Conches attributed the apparent elevation and depression of the planets to the influence of the sun, which dried them out—at some times more than at others—and caused them to rise. But when they drew more humors than usual from inferiors, the increased weight presumably made them descend.[51] The difficulty in such an ex-

48. Honorius, *De imagine mundi,* 1, iii; *MP, 172,* col. 121.

49. Although this explanation still had some validity in the later thirteenth century; it was offered by Albertus Magnus in *De generatione,* Bk. 2, tractate 2, ch. ii, in A. Borgnet, ed., *Opera omnia* (hereafter referred to as *OO*) (38 vols. Paris, Vivès, 1890–1900), *4,* col. 428.

50. Adelard of Bath, *Quaestiones naturales,* ch. lxiv, Eng. trans. Israel Gollancz, *Dodi-Ve-Nechdi* (Oxford, Oxford University Press, 1920), pp. 148–50.

51. William of Conches, *De philosophia mundi,* 2, xxiii; *MP, 172,* cols. 64–65.

planation, of course, lies in "at times" and "more than usual."
Very often such a difficulty was concealed by a spurious analogy;
the sun was pulled along by the firmament just as a small object
alongside is pulled by a ship.[52] The extremes to which a twelfth-
century scientist might go to get a purely physical explanation
of events is illustrated by William's explanation of tides: he
posited a fountain of water in the midst of the torrid (and hence
unobservable) zone which squirted water east and west. These
streams of water flowed on until they came to the east or west,
as the case might be, and then each parted, so that there were
then four streams, two flowing north and two south, "following
the sides of the earth." Naturally when they got to the north
or south they bumped into each other and fell back—hence the
tides.[53] Such a prodigious fountain already predicated for waves,
by the mere principle of economy might also account for the
winds. When the water flowing from the fountain got to its
lateral limits, it stirred up the air. This stirred-up air might move
toward the center, making eastern and western winds, or it might
follow the water around the corners to the north and south until
it came to be deflected—this time, to the south or north, across
the lands unknown to William in either case.[54] Apparently nothing whatsoever happened on the backside of the world. Hence
William accounted for the four cardinal winds. The winds William
called "coordinate," those between the cardinal points of the compass (and apparently there were just four of them), resulted from
one or another of these currents along the sides of the earth being
slowed down "from a certain accident."[55]

Although it is easy to dismiss such speculations as characteristic
medieval aberrations, they were serious hypotheses offered by
thoughtful men to account for real phenomena in the world.
Adelard was simply too confident in naïve analogy; this confidence
was as characteristic a trait of the Middle Ages as of the classical
period.[56] But William was betrayed by the same habit of mind

52. Ibid., xxv; *MP, 172,* col. 66.
53. Ibid., 3, xiv; *MP, 172,* col. 80. The theory was of course derived
from Macrobius, *Dream of Scipio,* 2, ix; pp. 214–15.
54. William of Conches, *De philosophia mundi,* 3, xv; *MP, 172,* cols.
81–82.
55. Ibid.
56. See Cornford, *The Laws of Motion,* passim.

we saw in Isidore. He was looking for the origin of action and change in a particular body; he was thinking of action or movement as an attribute of a body. When the action or movement was so clearly visible, as with the tides, it seemed safe enough to predicate a corresponding body, a monstrous fountain, to account for it.

But these pseudo-mechanical explanations did not take twelfth-century science very far, and most of the gross physical events of the world were explained in another way, by reference to the elements themselves. For example, the heat that the sun manifestly extended to the earth was something of a problem, since it was a property of fire, and hence of heat, to rise above the air, not to descend through it. William explained this by contiguity: the air, being under the fire, was warmed by it, and the earth and sea were in turn warmed by the air.[57] But such an explanation could not be very satisfactory in the twelfth century, whose scientists always tended to think of elemental properties as associated with elements. Hence later, when William directly confronted the problem of the sun's heat, he fell back upon the principle of the mixture of elements. The sun, mixed as everything else, contains particles of earth and water, and these naturally seek to join the main bodies. (The principle, "like attracts like," available in Isidore and Macrobius,[58] could always be drawn upon by a medieval thinker; it was used habitually by Albertus Magnus[59]). But in so doing, these earthy and watery particles draw fiery particles along with them. Then the heat returns to the sun, by the same principle, and it draws water and earth back with it, again gratuitously.[60]

Heat, one of the qualities of fire (with dryness), is brought down from the sun, and moisture, or wetness, one quality of water, returns to it. In such an explanation one sees not merely the unaccountable operation of an elemental mixture; one sees the incipient dissolution of the elements themselves. On the basis of one passage in the *De philosophia mundi*, Duhem attributes to

57. William of Conches, *De philosophia mundi*, I, xxii–xxiii; *MP*, 172, cols. 55–56.
58. Isidore, *Etymologies*, 4, ix, 4. Macrobius, *Dream of Scipio*, 2, xv; p. 234.
59. For example, in *De generatione*, 2, 3, iv; col. 418.
60. William of Conches, *De philosophia mundi*, 3, v; *MP*, 172, col. 76.

William a conception of an element as "an indivisible atom."[61] William did indeed make such an assertion. But in practice the dissolution of the elements was for William a major explanatory technique. The stuff of the universe was not elements but qualities. One sees the possibilities in William's explanation for the fact that there were no stars in the air, although the air contained the same mixture of qualities as were responsible for the stars of the fiery region. He says, quoting Constantine the African,[62]

> As there are these four, and two qualities in each one, each has one characteristic from itself, another from another. Fire is hot from itself, dry from earth; air is moist from itself, hot from fire; water is cold from itself, moist from air; earth is dry from itself, but is cold from water. But in each one, that which is from itself prevails more than that which is from another.

Such an explanation virtually identifies each element with one specific quality; the other quality becomes little more than an accident.

Hence more phenomena are explained by William of Conches in terms of qualitative change than in any other way. Bloody rains, for instance, were simply rains that had been inflamed by heat and then thickened.[63] Salt water was water that had been thickened by the sun, since it was "exceedingly certain" that water passed into salt upon being boiled; this salt water could be sweetened by being "squeezed out" and thinned by underground cataracts.[64] Lightning was heated air which, because of motion, had passed into "a fiery substance," or perhaps it was "air burning and gleaming from a blow."[65]

William of Conches was committed to an explanation of how things happened in the world of nature and made a sharp assault on those who were too hasty in their recourse to the will of God: "For we say that a reason ought to be sought for everything."[66]

61. Duhem, Le Système, 3, 103.
62. De philosophia mundi, 1, xxi; MP, 172, col. 55.
63. Ibid., vii; MP, 172, col. 77.
64. Ibid., xvi; MP, 172, col. 82.
65. Ibid., x; MP, 172, col. 78.
66. Ibid., 1, xxii; MP, 172, col. 56.

Supernatural explanations ought to be reserved for those events, like comets,[67] which flatly contradicted the laws of nature. But William's explanations were sought according to preexistent and usually unconscious assumptions about the general nature of movement and change in moving and changing objects. This Isidorean tendency is very clearly seen in the explanation for falling stars, which were always troublesome to medieval scientists, because things could not happen where these events seemed to be taking place:[68]

> Seeing that often in the higher parts of the air there is wind and commotion, even though it is not in the lower parts, from that moving about, ignited and flowing air runs through the air. Which when it begins to shine near any star, the sight of that star is borne to us by its brightness, and it seems that the star has fallen. But someone may say, whence is it then that we do not see that star? To which we say: that that same star is seen by us afterward, but we do not recognize it to be the same. For when, as we said before, fiery air runs about, thicker and hence slower air follows after, which being placed between us and that star, blocks off its sight from us. But before it may pass, and the star appear, the firmament, which revolves toward setting, bears off that star with it to the regions beyond. And when it appears, because it is seen in another place than it was, it is thought to be another star.

This passage describes a series of essentially unique changes which, by their uniqueness, became properties of objects. There is the air ignited by movement (unquestionably a change in substance in the medieval view); there is the fiery air illuminating a star but not, apparently, itself visible; there is the mysteriously thickened air being drawn after the thinner air; and finally there is this thicker air obscuring light. In trying to explain this mysterious appearance, William was led to posit two substantial changes in air, which in fact became two different substances.

67. Ibid., 3, xii; *MP, 172,* col. 80.
68. Ibid., xii; *MP, 172,* col. 79; amended by the text of Bede, *Opera, MP, 90,* col. 1163.

At the same time, motion and change were conceptualized in a thoroughly Isidorean spirit: they began and then stopped. This is handsomely illustrated by a short passage on the nature of rains:[69]

> Hence there are various causes for rains. For at times a thick and humid fume evaporates, which when it ascends the most minute drops collect around each other, and being made larger, fall, and a rain takes place. But at times the air from coldness of the earth and water is thickened and passes into a watery substance, which being dissolved by the heat of the sun, as ice by fire, falls as small particles. At times the sun draws moisture to feed its luster (*coloris*), and that which is more liquid in it passes into a fiery substance. But that which is heavier falls down, whence we see that after the most acute heat an inundation of rain takes place.

There is no frame of reference in which individual activities may be understood; each action appears moved by unfathomable internal principles, and each action was finally as unique to William of Conches as were the objects he considered.

The Aristotelian Revival of the Thirteenth Century

The thirteenth century did not merely recover the commentaries of Aristotle; it recovered at the same time the opinions of his predecessors imbedded in the Aristotelian text, and it inherited the commentaries of the Arabs who had been the trustees of the inheritance. The scientists of the age generally felt obliged to deal with all opinions relevant to any particular topic, and this resulted in an immense amount of thirteenth-century writing on physical theory. Fortunately for the present study, we need only note the effect of this Aristotelianism by an examination of general attitudes toward nature. This can be done in reasonable compass.

There is a rough analogy between the impact of Aristotle in the fourth century B.C. and his impact upon the thirteenth century A.D.; in both eras his significance lay in his solutions to prob-

69. Ibid., 3, iv; *MP*, *172*, col. 76; and Bede, *Opera*, *MP*, *90*, col. 1161.

lems of motion. The twelfth century, to be sure, was bare of any knowledge of the dilemma of Parmenides, and hence Aristotle did not come upon the scene to resolve a generally recognized difficulty. Rather, he offered a truly methodical system for accounting for motion and change. The notion that the universe was comprehensible in its workings was abroad in the twelfth century, even if the rationalistic spirit of William of Conches was not universally admired by his contemporaries.[70] We can see an effort to systematize the understanding of nature in the works of William, Honorius, Bernard Sylvester, and Alexander Neckham. But these efforts can hardly be called successful. Twelfth-century explanations of natural phenomena remained ad hoc. They were improvisations that depended on uncertain assumptions about astronomy and the elements and were stuck together with principles derived from common knowledge and analogy. Medieval science never wholly lost this ad hoc quality, of course, but Aristotle offered a ready-made system of scientific explanation, self-consistent far beyond anything envisioned in the twelfth century. The scientists of the thirteenth century could thus aim at a system of physical explanation that would be perfectly homogeneous, with the same principles operating throughout.[71]

But the Aristotelian revival had a further important consequence: it established as a fundamental and fully conscious premise the principle that the state of rest was the natural condition of any body in the universe. In this matter, of course, the medieval Aristotelians outran the master. Aristotle had only asserted that the natural state of any sublunary body was a state of rest; in his locus classicus on the subject, the twelfth book of the *Metaphysics*,[72] he provided independent movers for every heavenly body, giving them a natural movement independent of that of the great sphere encircling the whole universe and communicating to it its

70. For a dissenting view see the *De erroribus Guillelmi de Conchis* by William of St. Thierry, *MP, 180,* cols. 334–40.

71. At the beginning of the *Meteororum,* Albert provides a guide through his various commentaries upon the physical treatises of Aristotle. In his free reordering of the books of the various treatises he was actually aiming at a higher degree of order than Aristotle himself had proposed. *Meteororum,* 1, 1, ii; *OO, 4,* cols. 1–2.

72. Which was, of course, Book 11 in the medieval commentaries because these two books were transposed in the medieval translation.

primary movement, the primum mobile.[73] This opinion generated an extensive controversy in the Middle Ages about whether the orbs of the heavens possessed souls as well as intelligences, about the exact relationship that such souls and intelligences bore to their orbs, and about the identification of these classical entities with Christian angels.[74] It was a controversy, in other words, about the nature of the dependence of these secondary orbs upon the Prime Mover. No medieval Aristotelian, as far as I have observed, conceded to such orbs and their movers anything but a mediating function, and hence the orbs implicitly fell into the class of objects dependent upon the primum mobile and ultimately upon the Prime Mover. In its deepest implications the new controversy was merely a very old one disguised—the controversy between Platonic emanations and Christian providence.[75]

73. Aristotle, *Metaphysics,* Bk. 12, ch. viii, 1073a–1074b, 14, ed. and trans. Hugh Tredennick (2 vols. Cambridge, Mass., Loeb Classical Library, 1936), 2, 152–63. W. D. Ross, *Aristotle* (5th ed. London, 1949), p. 98, points out that the independence of these secondary movers could hardly have been very satisfactory to Aristotle himself.

74. Albertus reviews current problems arising from the Aristotelian texts in his commentary on the *Metaphysics* (*Metaphysicorum libri XIII,* Bk. 11, tractate 2; *OO, 6,* 609 ff.). Albertus plumps for the dependency of all things upon the first cause without, apparently, regarding it as an opinion that needs any defense (Ibid., ch. xxi, pp. 644–45). Indeed, he specifically attributes the opinion that secondary movers were independent to *senioribus et antiquissimis,* and he calls it an opinion which *dimissum est a posterioribus* (Ibid., ch. xxix, p. 657). Saint Thomas Aquinas, at least in his commentary upon the *Metaphysics,* seems to be unaware that Aristotle's text implies independence for the first movers (*Commentary on the Metaphysics of Aristotle,* Eng. trans. John P. Rowan [2 vols. Chicago, Regnery, 1961], 2, 898–99). And, although the condemnation of 1277 deals with Aristotle's theory of multiple causation as it appears in the passage under consideration (P. Mandonnet, *Siger de Brabant et l'averroisme latin au xiiime siècle* [2 vols. Louvain, Institut supérieur de philosophie de l'Université, 1908], 2, 178–79), the writer against whom the condemnations seem to have been principally addressed, Siger, does not seem to have held any such opinions (Fernand Van Steenberghen, *Aristotle in the West* [Louvain, E. Narwelaerts, 1955], p. 223). There seems to me at least reason to doubt that a medieval writer of any consequence followed Aristotle in this rather surprising view.

75. Duhem, it seems to me, takes much too seriously the disparity between different passages on this subject in the writings of Albertus. He argues that the passage in the *Sentences* (*Commentarii in secundum librum sententiarum,* Dist. XIV, c, art 6; *OO, 27,* 265–66) represents Albertus' real thought on the subject. But the passage in question simply

It is not surprising that the Aristotelian view of the heavens should have been passed by; the dependence of the whole universe for its activity upon the will of God, however described, was a premise fundamental to many medieval conflicts. It was precisely the necessity for such a dependence that made Free Will such a problem in Augustinian thought. It is more surprising, perhaps, that the application of this principle to medieval physical theory should have been mediated by Aristotle.

Yet, prior to the Aristotelian revival, the fact that a monotheistic universe might best be served by a regular order of physical causes seems not to have been clearly grasped. William of Conches illustrates this habit of mind:[76]

> The bodies of stars having been created, they began to move themselves, and by this motion to warm the supporting air, but with the air mediating water was warmed. From the warm water various kinds of animals were created, of which those which had more of the higher elements were birds.

William did not mean to eliminate the Creator in this passage; elsewhere he proved the existence of God by the argument from design.[77] But he did not realize that so fundamental a problem as the initiation of all motion and change might require some sort of explanation. This sort of naïveté was no longer possible after the rediscovery of Aristotle. The principle that dominated thirteenth-century scientific thought was ordinarily quoted from the opening

---

affirms, in the spirit of St. Bernard, that the heavens are moved by the Divine Will. Of course they were moved by the Divine Will. The medieval question was, "How?" And if this question were not admitted, the whole scholastic endeavor was in manifest error, since it was fundamentally directed to the understanding of the "how" of God's will. In my judgment, the commentaries on the *Sentences* are much less reliable a guide to Albertus' opinion than his Aristotelian commentaries, which are anything but a slavish explication of Aristotle, as Duhem, *Système, 6,* 440–50, avers. Albertus was not utterly consistent, as the following pages will show, but the opinions he expressed in his Aristotelian commentaries are clearly his own.

76. William of Conches, *De philosophia mundi,* i, xxii; *MP, 172,* col. 55.

77. Ibid., v; *MP, 172,* cols. 44–45.

of the seventh book of the *Physics:* "everything that is moved is moved by something."[78] The thirteenth century hoped to formulate a system explaining the world based upon this principle.

The first necessity in such a system, in the thirteenth century as well as in the Aristotelian context, was the postulation of a Prime Mover, immobile, ingenerable, and unalterable, whose function was to counter the innate tendencies of the universe to quiescence, and who was able to do this because He was essentially outside nature. And the sole function of this Prime Mover was, of course, to generate the motion of the primum mobile.[79]

In theory, perhaps, all motion and change depended ultimately upon this primum mobile. Robertus Anglicus, in his commentary on the *Sphere* of Sacrobosco, asserted that if it should ever stop, the whole universe would be instantly "congealed."[80] But in practice, and in the ordinary thought of the thirteenth-century scientist, the primum mobile provided a second principle of motion; the first was the innate tendencies of the elements to seek their own place. "Why the elements do not remain separated from each other in their own places" is a chapter title in the *De Generatione* of Albertus Magnus[81] which implies the real function of the primum mobile: to generate some sort of counterforce to insure continuing activity of all kinds.

But there was still a major obstacle to this understanding of change: How could this essentially exterior force, uniform and in every way undifferentiated, explain the immense variety in heavenly and terrestrial phenomena? The difficulties are apparent in Albertus' explanation of the creation of the world by the action of this primum mobile. It begins with a medieval version of

78. Usually quoted from the *Physica,* Bk. 7, ch. i; 241b (*The Physics,* ed. and trans. Philip Wicksteed and Francis Cornford [London and Cambridge, Mass., Loeb Classical Library, 1934], 2, 207–11). However, it is also to be found in the *De coelo,* Bk. 2, ch. vi; 288a (*On the Heavens,* trans. W. K. C. Guthrie [Cambridge, Mass., Loeb Classical Library, 1935], p. 171).

79. See Albertus, *De meteororum,* 1, 1, iv; *OO, 4,* 480–81.

80. John of Sacrobosco, *The Sphere of Sacrobosco and its Commentators,* ed. Lynn Thorndike (Chicago, University of Chicago Press, 1949), p. 157.

81. Albertus, *De generatione et corruptione,* 2, 2, vii; *OO, 4,* 452.

friction; any rapid movement by one body adjacent to another produces heat (by a method which we will shortly examine[82]); the greater the moving body and the thinner the adjacent body, the greater the heat. Hence an area of intense heat was produced immediately under the primum mobile. The area was dry as well, because heat in its greatest intensity burns up moisture (*quia calidum in excellentia est totum adurens humidum*) the area was of course the region of fire. Air, being hot and moist, was created in the next region; the heat there wasn't great enough either to drive out the moisture or to burn it up. Water had the next place for obvious reasons: being at a sufficient remove, it was "allowed to be" cold.[83]

> Lastly, that which retreats wholly from the orb and the effect of its motion is resting, and has cold in its virtue, which so presses upon the parts of matter that it squeezes all natural humidity from them. And this is cold and dry, in its virtue, and it is called earth.

This is surely an explanation of creation as unsatisfactory as the parallel attempt of William of Conches. The motion of the primum mobile did not create the elements of the world; both water and earth, implicitly, were already there. Cold, in medieval theory, was not the absence of heat; it was an element, with as much positive reality as fire itself had; it was solid enough to "squeeze" the natural humidity from matter.

This difficulty is still more apparent in the incessant attempts that Albertus made to specify the way in which natural processes were continually dependent upon the primum mobile. In the first place, there was the difficulty of translating regular movement to irregular movement. This difficulty was resolved rather neatly by recourse to a major perplexity of the Ptolemaic account of the heavens, the apparently oblique motion of the zodiac and the planets within its limits. The primum mobile, according to Albertus, transmitted its regular motion to the zodiac, which was

---

82. See below, p. 29. Isidore had attributed lightning to the rubbing together of clouds. *Etymologies,* 13, ix, 1.

83. Albertus, *De meteororum,* 1, 1, vii; *OO, 4,* 485. A similar explanation is found in *De coelo,* 2, 3, v; *OO, 4,* 177–78.

also regular with respect to the primum mobile. But it was irregular with respect to the earth, since its orbit was not parallel to the earth's equinoctial.[84] Hence regularity might be translated into irregularity essentially and not accidentally—and this was an important consideration.

Here was the beginning of a realization of the great objective of thirteenth-century science, to show how, "for all inferior things, the order of causes hangs from a superior order." But the attempt ended in an understanding of causation exactly analogous to the theory of causation of the twelfth century, with discrete objects moving, or behaving, discretely.

Albertus' evidence for the significance of zodiacal obliquity to earthly change was, of course, the seasons, which he distinguished from one another at least as sharply as William of Conches had done. ("The sun having come to the point of Aries . . . generation begins to be."[85]) But how was this motion, irregular though it might be, capable of becoming a causal principle for the multifarious courses that living things pursue? One would have expected the seasons to become an intermediary principle between zodiac and terrestrial generation. Such was not Albertus' explanation, and one sees the characteristic medieval bent toward direct and limited influences. He attached each case of generation and corruption directly to the zodiacal movement by means of what he called "periods." A period he defined as "a measure which is imprinted on, or flows from, the heavenly circle, as a thing caused by the circle, on inferiors."[86] An example of such a period working, and a kind of evidence for it, was a certain fish, the *dies* or *ediurna,* which normally lived exactly twenty-four hours. The period of this fish was obviously determined by the annual rotation of the sun, together with the movement of the planets and the zodiac itself. But this kind of regularity, in which the generation and corruption of earthly things was directly attached to the cycles of the heavenly bodies, was hardly sufficient as a general explanation because, as Albertus himself pointed out, in that case everything (except the *dies,* of course) would die in winter. So he pro-

84. Albertus, *De generatione,* 2, 3, iv; *OO, 4,* 448–49. See also *De meteororum,* 1, 1, iv; *OO, 4,* 481.

85. Ibid.

86. Albertus, *De generatione,* 2, 3, iv; *OO, 4,* 450.

posed an extended definition, by which the period became the measure

> made by the *relatio* of an ascending sign above the horizon
> to all the other signs of the circle with their stars and planets
> in the hour of the conception or the nativity of an inferior
> thing which is created or jointly caused by the heavenly circle.
> For in this way the measure of certain things is the year, and
> of other things is more or less, according to the effect of the
> signs and of the strength of the stars which are fixed in the
> signs. And in this way the time of generation of a thing is
> equal to the time of corruption.[87]

In this way the virtue originating in the primum mobile was converted into very nearly an infinity of virtues, each moving from a specific point to a specific point in effect, each conferring upon its recipient a unique cycle of generation and corruption. Nor did Albertus see anything remarkable in this state of affairs; in a subsequent discussion he shows himself to have been much more interested in the fact that the period of generation equalled the period of corruption than in this marvelous—and mysterious—derivation of the many from the one.

The same frame of reference (having the same consequence) is apparent in the second problem presented by the primum mobile, the generation of different kinds of forces, or virtues, from one unvarying movement. Such generation was necessary in view of the fact that movement and change of inanimate objects had to be reduced to the interaction of the four elements and their constituent qualities. In the order of cause and effect, as in the order of creation, everything began, according to Albertus, with the generation of heat by the medieval version of friction, by the rubbing of the primum mobile upon the unformed matter beneath. At least upon one occasion this was explained by the fact that such friction reduced adjacent matter to the smallest possible particle size; this brought about the fiery zone, since fire was simply the smallest particles, as earth was the largest.[88] But this was not

---

87. Ibid., pp. 450–51.
88. Albertus, *De coelo*, 2, 3, i; *OO, 4,* 168–69. See also *De meteororum,* 1, 1, xi; *OO, 4,* 489–90.

the only consequence of the motion of the outer limits of the universe; it also stimulated the sun and "certain stars" to generate heat, and it stimulated the sun, and only the sun, to generate light (the light from other celestial bodies was reflected from the sun). But this light of the sun was in turn manifestly warming to the objects upon which it fell. Hence, the primum mobile provided three separate and distinct sources of heat.

Here was a mystery—in fact, two mysteries. It was a mystery that heat should generate light in the first place and a mystery that light should in turn generate heat, as it did particularly in the case of the sun. Let us take up the second first. Light was able to generate heat in three circumstances: through nearness, through refraction, and through *architudo,* when the sun in its ellipse lingers in approximately the same celestial position for a period of time. Albertus points out that it lingered in this way over Ethiopia and thus explains the excessive heat of that place. But none of these observations, it is clear, really attempted to explain how light generated heat. They merely proposed certain circumstances in which this transformation might take place. What we have in reality is nature whose essence is a capacity for spontaneous change. Technically, according to Albertus, the heat generated by light remained an accident of that light. But such heat was nevertheless a new substance of sorts, generated out of light to which it bore no visible relationship. Albertus did not even attempt to explain this generation; he only specified the circumstances under which it was observed.[89]

The same ultimate mystery, this time located specifically in the nature of a body, is observed in Albertus' explanation of why only the light of the sun has the capacity to heat. Part of the explanation is obvious and unremarkable: the unique magnitude and thickness of the sun made it rub more vigorously upon the matter below it, and this rubbing generated heat by friction. But part of the explanation is not obvious: the sun was able to heat by its light because its light was "more pressing down" than the light of the other stars, and the subtlety and purity of its substance made its light "more penetrating and dissolving." Here we are obviously dealing with a unique substance and its unique quality.[90]

89. Ibid., 2, 3, iii; *OO, 4,* 172–73.
90. Ibid.

A further characteristic of the sun, according to "certain philosophers" whom Albertus does not seem inclined to contradict, was that it had "in the nature of its light" the capacity to move water, and the light of the other five planets had the capacity to move air.[91] These peculiar capacities are simply asserted. They are perhaps clarified, if not explained, by a passage in which Albertus undertook to explain why the light of the stars is not hot, although they receive this light from the sun (an Aristotelian doctrine). Albertus explains that the planets and fixed stars receive the light of the sun in their interiors, where such light is converted to the nature of the individual planets particularly, or to the stars in general. Hence such light generates not heat, but cold, or wet, or whatever.[92] But this is an incredible transformation. The reduction of all qualities of force to the primum mobile through the sun does not generalize the notion of force; such forces remain as unique, finally, in the system of Albertus as they were in the ancient *Etymologies*.

There is no need to rehearse here the familiar matter–form thesis of Aristotle that was taken over in its entirety by the thirteenth century. By this Aristotelian hypothesis, both constituents of things, matter and form, could become explanatory of change, since the change induced by form always presumed a potentiality for such change already existent in matter. The view[93] that potentiality was Aristotle's fundamental contribution to the physical theory of St. Thomas and Albertus seems doubtful to me; potentiality as a property of matter would be important only to an age for whom the Parmenidean problem of change from one state to another is very real, and the early Middle Ages was surely not such a time. The real function of potentiality in the thirteenth century was rather to explain, if "explain" be taken broadly, phenomena which could not otherwise be accounted for. This function is apparent in Albertus' account of how the virtues of the heavenly bodies manifest themselves in terrestrial phenomena. Life-spans ruled by periods should be predictably regular, and they

91. Ibid.

92. Ibid., 1, 1, xi; *OO, 4,* 35; see also *De generatione,* 2, 3, v; *OO, 4,* 450.

93. James A. Weisheipl, *The Development of Physical Theory in the Middle Ages* (New York, Sheed, 1960), p. 37.

should be divisable into equal segments of generation and corruption. But this is manifestly not the case. So Albertus appealed to differences in the capacity of matter to receive and maintain forms —in short, to discrepancies in potentiality.[94] Thus the Aristotelian theory of potentiality was the last link in the explanatory system stretching between the undifferentiated state of the unmoved mover and the extreme variety of terrestrial phenomena. It was, of course, an explanatory principle that could be guaranteed in advance to explain anything. At the same time, this potentiality of matter was thoroughly in accord with the spirit of the other causal explanations; it merely reinforced the uniqueness of objects and the uniqueness of actions and change.

This understanding of natural events pervaded Albertus' whole system. For example, the various meteorological phenomena— hail, rain, snow, and so forth—were to be explained by the heat of the sun "calling forth, igniting" a vapor from water.[95] (In the same passage he speaks of heat imprinting "its species" upon water.) This vapor was essentially distinct from water, midway between water and air, "having in itself something of the matter and form and act of air." In short, there was a change in substance, and it was this change that was responsible for the change of place. This new substance, having acquired something of the substance of air, sought the place of air. If the heat were sufficient, such a vapor might finally be converted to fire; if less, it might become air. But an "accidental coldness . . . which interfering clutches and thickens and converts," might reverse the process, with the vapor reverting to the cold and wet of moisture.[96] Common meteorological phenomena were deduced from such accidental reversions. Coldness operating unchecked brought about hail, frost, and rainstorms. But dew was the result of a sort of impasse, when cold pressed together and heat dissolved simultaneously.[97]

Hence we find the whole physical theory of the greatest physical theorist of the thirteenth century pervaded by an explanation of motion and change that, in spite of the new terminology and in

94. Albertus, *De generatione*, 2, 3, v; *OO*, 4, 450–51.
95. Albertus, *De meteororum*, 2, 1, ii; *OO*, 4, 520.
96. Ibid.
97. Ibid., 2, 1, i; *OO*, 4, 520. See 1, 4, ix; *OO*, 4, 515–16, for essentially the same procedures applied to the disturbances in the region of fire.

spite of the systematization made possible by Aristotle, was essentially no different from the unsystematic explanations offered by William of Conches. The drive for an embracing system did not unify the fragmented universe of earlier centuries; if anything, the entities of the universe became, in the theorizing of Albertus, even more discrete, even more self-sufficing, than they had been earlier.

Isidore was so dominated by the discreteness of objects that movement and change were very secondary considerations, and they were naturally located in objects when they did come under consideration. But Albertus was quite consciously working from a first premise locating action in objects. He insisted upon the priority of substantial change in sublunar alteration, and to this end he posited in each of the four elements a potentiality to become any one of the other three.[98] An element in inanimate nature could not alter its position with respect to the elemental structure of the universe; first there had to be a change in the substance of the element. Water, for instance, could not occupy the place of air until it had changed its nature and became a kind of air.[99]

This extreme of locating movement and change in objects in turn reinforced the discreteness of objects. Over and over Albertus must posit an object to explain an action. In the meteorological explanations noted above, for instance, the essence of the explanation was a fifth element, in effect, an airy substance which was neither water nor air. In his explanation of the various kinds of "great fires" which terrified the population from time to time, he described a *chasmata* as taking place when "a much-inflamed vapor, subtle and rare, is in a watery cloud of exceeding thinness."[100] This watery cloud with its contents is surely as strange a phenomenon as the hollowed-out receptacle of Alexander Neckham. Similarly, Albert explained the fact that large rivers arise in mountainous regions by positing places within these mountains which drew water by their heat, "just as dry sponges."[101] Here we find not only unique places, but places with unique characteristics; these hot spots in the normally cold and dry earth

98. Ibid., 1, 1, iv; *OO, 4,* 481.
99. Ibid., vi; *OO, 4,* 483–84.
100. Ibid., 1, 4, ix; *OO, 4,* 515.
101. Ibid., 2, 2, vii; *OO, 4,* 551.

were as gratuitously and eccentrically presupposed as anything in the *Etymologies* of Isidore; they were justified only by the necessity of having an object to serve as an appropriate point of origin for an action.

The medieval view of nature generally held between the time of Isidore and the time of Albertus was the same, in spite of the enormous increase in knowledge, because of the constancy of presuppositions about the fundamental construction of the universe and the way in which objects behave. These presuppositions limited man's understanding of nature for a much longer period of time than this. Isidore's view was not much different from that of Pliny; the same view of nature persisted for some centuries past the time of Albertus, even if there is debate about its terminus. Although it was not confined to the Middle Ages, this was the medieval view of nature, and it was a dominant perceptual framework in England throughout the fourteenth and fifteenth centuries. If the scientists of the fourteenth century, like Jean Buridan and Nicholas of Oresme, actually transcended the limits of medieval scientific thought outlined here, their view of nature did not provide the educated man with a new framework of beliefs. The ideas of Isidore and Albertus provided the conceptual framework within which all kinds of activities were ordered and, in some sense, understood.

The Medieval View of Nature as a System

The thinkers of the twelfth and thirteenth centuries were defeated by their unconscious presuppositions. They visualized the physical universe as a field of objects, of discrete points; they attributed the activity and change visible on every side in this universe to forces, or virtues, located initially within one or another of these objects. As a consequence, the most profound feeling for order in the Middle Ages was spatial, and, inevitably, geometric—a framework of discrete points connected by forces that were straight lines running between them. This way of looking at physical events and attempting to understand them extended to other matters; it is no accident that whenever a conceptual difficulty presented itself, a medieval writer was likely to draw a geometric figure to illuminate it. Even the medieval ethical system was presented as geometry, a system of paired opposites connected by lines of force (humility as a remedy for pride, for example) and appeared in the margins of manuscripts in geometric form.

The best way to visualize this medieval order is to see it as a series of superimposed geometric figures. The basic figure was the square; from this figure arose the fundamental medieval reliance upon the related opposites of hot and cold, wet and dry, the elements, the humors which corresponded to the elements, and so forth. Superimposed upon this square was a twelve-sided figure, and a seven-sided one as well, for the zodiac and its planets were of immense significance. The figure would have to be fantastically complicated to include the hours of the day, the days of the week, and the other divisions medieval thinkers were inclined to cherish.[102] Some further place would perhaps have to be provided for a ten-sided, or perhaps a second seven-sided, figure to provide for the numerology inherited from Macrobius and others, although this consideration generally remained theoretical and literary.[103]

The notion of force did nothing to simplify this complexity; the universe was run, not by a force, but by a multitude of different forces. The theologian might refer everything to God, and the scientist might strive mightily for a monistic universe by making all power ultimately astrological, but each in his ordinary, unpro-

---

102. Alexander Neckham provides many examples of this medieval habit of geometrizing everything in sight. See Bk. I, ch. xi ff., of the *De natura rerum,* in which the hours of the day are apportioned to the planets, in contempt of any conceivable physical relationship between these hours and planetary positions. *De natura rerum,* ed. T. Wright (London, Longmans, 1863), pp. 48 ff. This text is found in the Rolls Series, No. 34, *Rerum britannicarum medii aevi scriptores* [hereafter referred to as *RS*] (244 vols. London, Longmans, 1858–96). Chaucer espouses the same sort of system in his *A Treatise on the Astrolabe,* Bk. 2, para. 12 (*The Complete Works of Geoffrey Chaucer,* ed. F. N. Robinson [Boston, Houghton Mifflin Co., 1933], p. 650), and he makes use of such a system in *The Knight's Tale.* A major source for this kind of geometrizing was, of course, Macrobius.

103. Certain numbers, such as three and seven, were felt to have some sort of occult power inhering in them in some circumstances. A major difficulty in evaluating the significance of such material is the medieval habit of systematizing everything. The fact that some special significance was felt to accrue to Friday, for instance, led inevitably to the annunciation of comparable meanings for all the days of the week.

fessional thought, visualized the world as multifarious in its modes of operation. Such a visualization was inevitable. The very fact that this mysterious stuff, this power or virtue, inhered in objects and was diverse and even contradictory at times in its operations made it impossible to visualize it otherwise than as in itself diverse —as plural rather than singular. One might explain the influence of Saturn by its wetness, but wetness and Saturn remained distinct (particularly since the qualitative accounts of the planets often included such nonelemental things as benignity).[104] The virtues of stones might be related to astrology, but these virtues, once achieved, were distinct from astrological virtues.[105] The multiplicity of virtues is particularly apparent in medieval medicine. The elemental qualities of hot, cold, wet, and dry were of course basic in the theoretical accounts of herbs, but the virtue of a particular herb was not subsumed by theory; the virtue of an herb, its power or force, was unique.[106]

To make matters even more desperate, there were loose in the universe endless numbers of forces lying quite outside the usual "systematic" account of the way things happened. It was very easy to point to occult virtues—the power to draw iron to itself was an occult virtue of the magnet—but it was not so easy to define them. An occult virtue was probably any power inhering in a substance which was not due to the elemental qualities of that

104. Jupiter, for instance, is described as benevolent by William of Conches, *De philosophia mundi*, 2, xvii; *MP*, 172, col. 62. Robertus Anglicus avoids this difficulty by splitting up the elemental qualities: Mars and the sun were both hot and dry, but the former was consuming, the latter life-giving (John of Sacrobosco, *The Sphere of Sacrobosco*, Lectio III, p. 155). This explanation is a good example of the nonchalance with which a medieval thinker could dissolve the fundamental stuff of his universe.

105. See, for example, the prayer found in the anonymous *Sur les propriétés des choses* quoted in "Traités divers sur les propriétés des choses," in *Histoire Litteraire de la France* (37 vols. Paris, 1888), 3, 371. In this little prayer for the restoration of occult virtue to a stone which has lost it, it is very clear that such virtues were independent of astrological influences, although, theoretically, of astrological origin.

106. Thus, over and over in the *Herbal of Rufinus*, pp. 126–27, 158, special properties were ascribed to herbs regardless of their essential composition. *Isopus*, according to the herbal *Circa instans* quoted by Rufinus, did not at all have the same range of application as *eruca*, although they both were hot and dry in the second degree.

substance. But St. Thomas asserted, if I read him correctly, that every mixture of elements had its own "specific form," not derived from its elements. The more noble the specific form, the more excellent the powers and operations arising from it.[107] Such a view made occult virtues nearly omnipresent in the universe and at the same time vitiated the power of medieval cosmology. Its explanatory techniques could never be applied with confidence in any particular instance.

Thorndike reports that there was an impulse in the later Middle Ages to abandon theory entirely in favor of a purely experiential concern with observable phenomena.[108] The wonder is that this impulse was not universal. Given the medieval hypotheses, a really systematic, coherent view of nature was impossible.

As a consequence, medieval attempts to explain a specific event or to argue for the possibility of a certain kind of phenomenon tended to be both ad hoc and analogic. The system was too loose to be of much explanatory or critical value, but there were parallels between natural activities, and these might serve.

The analogic system can be illustrated by a passage from William of Malmesbury's *Historia regum anglorum*. A man was assaulted by mice so persistently that his servants were not able to keep them off. They put the man into a boat and rowed out to sea, but nothing helped. The beasts, gnawing through the boards of the boat, forced them to turn back, and the unfortunate wretch, the only person attacked, was finally "entirely gnawed in pieces." William manfully defended the truth of this narrative by citing another marvel, so well substantiated as to be beyond dispute. Everyone knows, he pointed out, that "if a leopard should bite anyone, a party of mice immediately approaches to discharge their urine on the wounded man." If they succeed he dies, "but

107. Aquinas, *De occultis operibus naturae,* ed. and trans. Joseph McAllister, The Catholic University of America Philosophical Studies, 42 (Washington, Catholic University of America Press, 1939), p. 195; trans. p. 27. Aquinas attributed the power of amulets, charms, and so forth to demons. Thorndike has many discussions of occult virtues in his indispensable *History.* See, for instance, his discussion of occult virtues in the *De animalibus* of Albertus Magnus, *OO, 2,* 560–61.

108. See particularly his discussion of Nicholas Oresme's assault upon the idea of marvels (essentially occult virtues), an assault which depended heavily upon the notion that everything in the universe was equally marvelous. Thorndike, *History, 3,* 440–71.

if ... the destruction can be avoided during nine days, then medical assistance can be of value."[109]

William could regard the fact that mice approach people bitten by leopards to urinate on them as an invariable sequence in nature (particularly since he lived in England where leopards were scarce). The credibility of one event was established by comparing it to a parallel event that was a piece of the universal order. The evidence was purely analogic. Given the mysterious impulse that overcomes mice in the presence of leopard-bitten people (which was actually a kind of occult virtue), it was more probable that a man in a boat might call forth a comparable impulse. The two incidents have nothing else in common, even though one was proposed to confirm the veracity of the other.

These analogies have much in common with the physical theory of the time. Analogies and physical theory share an implicit triadal structure. Like the physical theory, they describe self-limiting actions originating in particular bodies and terminating in other bodies. Furthermore, these practical, analogic explanations required unique objects as a point of origin, as did the theoretical, scientific explanations. It was the virtue of mice to urinate upon somebody bitten by a leopard just as it was the virtue of fire to seek the highest place in the universe or, in other circumstances, to burn. In each case, the conceptual system finally required unique bodies to account for unique effects.

We can best understand the implications of the medieval view of nature by comparing it to the modern view. The modern sciences must be explicitly ruled out of such a comparison, however. The word "science" having become the most potent, the most magical, in the twentieth-century lexicon, it has inevitably been extended to cover (or shelter) the most disparate studies. In this century there is no "scientific view" of anything, and hence science is useless as a point of comparison, which must be, instead, the view of nature generally held by educated men in this century. This point of comparison is difficult, but perhaps it can be made to serve.

It is still widely assumed that the difference between medieval

109. William of Malmesbury, *De gestis regum anglorum*, Bk. 3, sects. 290–91; *RS* 90:2, 344–45.

and modern somehow has to do with allegiance to observable facts; that the modern world began when, for some mysterious reason, men began to look around them more carefully than they had done before.[110] This explanation is not merely inadequate; it is wrong. The medieval man saw very well those workings of nature that his intellectual frame of reference allowed him to perceive. The substantial technological progress made during the Middle Ages reflects accurate and purposive intelligence. Indeed, it might be argued more reasonably that it was precisely a concern for practical problems, based upon close observation of details, that was the medieval contribution to the history of science.[111]

The manifest deficiencies of medieval science did not arise from an excess of theory; they arose from the assumptions behind that theory. The Isidorean discussion of goats, quoted earlier, will serve nicely as a text. Isidore would surely have referred the constellation of physical and behavioral characteristics which made up his description of goats to their natura; like his successors—and predecessors—he found the word came easily to his tongue. But we translate this term as "nature" only at the risk of profoundly misunderstanding our sources. If, upon some unimaginable occasion, an educated man of the twentieth century should have occasion to speak of the nature of goats, he would mean, with Isidore, a constellation of physical and behavioral traits; but he would have in mind a different kind of constellation. Goat nature would be assumed on a priori grounds to be self-consistent. Given certain facts about goats—that they have long hair, are hoofed, and so forth—we can accept or reject further assertions on the basis of their consistency with what we know. We can always err in such a judgment, of course. The medieval conception of the natura of an individual thing—goat, planet, or civilization—did not permit the judgment in the first place, because it did not presume any sort of consistency among the elements of that natura.

110. See A. E. Burtt, *The Metaphysical Foundations of Modern Physical Science* (New York, Harcourt, Brace and Co., 1927), pp. 28–29, for a typical statement of this sort. At best, it is an explanation that explains nothing.

111. Lynn White, in his recent study, *Medieval Technology and Social Change* (Oxford, Oxford University Press, 1962), pp. 129–34, argues that the "power-lust" which is ordinarily associated with the seventeenth century can be found in the thirteenth.

But there is a further, and perhaps even more important, difference. When Isidore found in his sources the assertion:[112] "The panther is so called either because it is the friend of all animals except the dragon, or because it rejoices in the society of its own kind, and returns the same likeness of whatever it receives as friend," he of course had no criteria for rejecting it. But we can reject it out of hand without ever having heard of a panther. The reason we can do this is that for us "nature" has a double significance. It refers to the individual thing, but it also refers to the collections, classes, or species in which the individual may be grouped. These collectivities have their own sort of coherence. We are able to reject Isidore's statement about the panther because it is inconsistent with our conception of animals, or better, "animalness," and it is not static but dynamic, a conception not of qualities but of function.

This dynamic universe is fundamental to the modern approach to all of nature. To explain a particular thing is really to relate it to the physical world as *process.* Or, more precisely, it is to relate that particular to one or another of the interrelated processes which, in sum, comprise the framework within which all natural events are presumed to take place. To explain why fire burns is to relate this specific event to the chemical process which we see as embracing all things. To explain why men grow bald is perhaps a more complex matter, since it would first be necessary to select the most appropriate process for the explanation—chemical, biochemical, or physiological.

In any case, modern techniques of explanation are, in essence, methods of relating specific events to frameworks of expectation logically prior to any particular event, and these frameworks describe processes. Bertrand Russell has called these processes which underlie particularities "chains of causes."[113] I would prefer the term "causal processes," since "chain" implies a one-to-one relationship which surely, in the modern view, does not exist in nature at any level. Whatever the term one selects, a cause in this view is not a property but itself an event, a happening, and causation is a continuous process. Action and interaction comprise

112. Isidore, *Etymologies,* 12, ii, 8.
113. Bertrand Russell, *A History of Western Philosophy* (New York, Simon and Schuster, 1945), p. 833.

the stuff of the universe, and every momentary state is the product of all of the previous relationships within that particular causal process.

A medieval thinker, too, might generalize from the specific natura of a thing to a second kind of natura, the collectivities embracing individuals. But this natura also bore little relationship to modern nature. This medieval natura in its collective sense is ordinarily described by modern scholars in one of two ways. Some are apt to make much of the Neoplatonic doctrine of hierarchies; indeed, Etienne Gilson would have this to be *the* view of nature in the twelfth century.[114] There are several difficulties, aside from the paucity of texts, in viewing this hierarchical natura as a genuinely explanatory principle. It is ordinarily found in contexts which make it obvious that the writer had no great interest in the perceived physical world as such; this is particularly true of the pseudo-Dionysian texts and the *De divisione* naturae of John Scotus Erigena. Secondly, the hierarchies as applied to the physical world never constituted a system. Most important, the hierarchical natura could never explain anything because the relationships it proposed were vertical, not horizontal. The great chain of being, for instance, proposed to place all created things in a vertical order stretching from rocks to God. But we do not significantly explain anything when we place it in such an order. (When this great chain is turned on its side, however, when it becomes a horizontal order by being seen as a development in time, it permits genuine explanations. Much of man's behavior—his response to sudden falls, for instance—can be explained by evolution.)[115]

The second, fairly common use of natura as some sort of collective ground behind individual things simply identified it as the procreative force inhering in individual objects. "Natura is so called," wrote Isidore, "from that which makes anything to be born"—which included, of course, a lot of "anythings" we would

114. Etienne Gilson, *La Philosophie au moyen age* (Paris, Payot, 1944), p. 343.
115. I do not mean to say that an a priori system permits, or will permit, any sort of complete explanation. The point is that modern horizontal relationships permit explanation, perhaps because they permit perceived relationships.

by no means regard as subject to parturition.[116] William of Conches proposed a similar definition.[117] This conception of natura also had a long career in literature, notably in the presiding geniuses of Alanus of Lille and Geoffrey Chaucer's *Parliament of Fowls*. But again, natura as procreative force was not particularly serviceable to the explanation of anything but the courtly lover's resistance to ecclesiastical strictures on sex.[118]

In short, the concept of natura as an explicitly affirmed collectivity or ground could not operate in medieval literature in an explanatory way, and I have encountered no medieval writer attempting to relate specific phenomena to such abstract concepts. We are justified in concluding, then, that although such conceptions were in some sense believed, they were not fundamental convictions at this time, but rather part of the intellectual inheritance that made no important difference because it was not related to the world as medieval men perceived it.[119]

The effective, perceived natura as ground was, in fact, the framework of expectations—the modes of perception—which I have been engaged in explicating. This is proven by the fact that whenever a medieval thinker proposed to explain a natural event he reduced it to the triadic structure of ground–action–consequence.[120] This conception of natura as ground did provide some

116. Isidore, *Etymologies,* 11, i, 1.

117. At least, he is quoted by Vincent of Beauvais as defining nature as "a certain innate force in things producing like from like." *Speculum naturale,* 2, v; col. 82. I have not found the passage from which this statement is drawn in the printed texts.

118. See, for instance, the speech of "Genius" in the *Roman de la rose,* ll. 1950 ff., Eng. trans. Harry W. Robbins, *The Romance of the Rose* (New York, Dutton, 1962), pp. 413 ff.

119. This passage is, of course, an explicit application of the general principles advanced in the introduction, pp. xvi–xvii.

120. It should be remarked that this view of nature which I have explicated is entirely consonant with the most commonly quoted Aristotelian texts on the subject. Relevant texts have been collected by Father Joseph Marling, "The Order of Nature in the Philosophy of St. Thomas Aquinas," Doctoral Dissertation, Catholic University, 1934, pp. 1–8. Furthermore, Aristotle's four causes, which St. Thomas explicated as the "principles" of nature (*De Principiis naturae,* ed. John J. Pauson [Louvain, Fribourg, 1950]), also lent themselves to this triadal analysis. The present study does not, of course, presume to say anything about the Aristotelian view of nature.

sort of homogeneity for the physical universe, since it provided a basic pattern of activity which embraced all things. But it did not make for a perceptual unity, as unity is generally understood, because the basic pattern was one of severely circumscribed relationships among essentially unique objects and events. The net effect must have been to make human experience in nature discrete and fragmentary.

It is perhaps worth pointing out again that the intent of the foregoing comparison between medieval and modern conceptions of nature is explanatory and not evaluative. Comparison is a means to understanding, and there is no generally available conception of nature other than the modern to which the medieval might be conveniently compared. It would be hypocritical, of course, to pretend that I think the medieval view of nature was as serviceable, or as near the truth, as the modern. (When we praise medieval writers for views which we know to be wrong, it is impossible not to be patronizing, as it is impossible not to patronize bright children.) But superiority or inferiority is of no consequence. It is of consequence to be aware of the qualitative difference between the medieval and modern view, because such awareness helps us to understand ourselves. Medieval scientists saw nature through their perceptual framework. At some point between, probably, 1300 and 1500, a new perceptual framework made its appearance in Western Europe, and the modern understanding of nature is mediated by this new way of seeing. It is, however, still mediated.

The medieval view of nature did not exist in splendid isolation from other medieval ways of perception. It was a part of a total Weltanschauung. Causation in nature was a singular affair, depending upon the qualities of the object from which it arose. Causation in human affairs acted in much the same way. It is a major function of the balance of this study to demonstrate the relationship between the perception of action and actors in the natural world and those in the human world.

CHAPTER 2

Perception of Human Action:
The Clerical Chronicles

The writer of the Middle Ages engaged in recording human happenings had several alternatives available to him (although his selection was determined by forces beyond his control). He could list, narrate, or explain. All three approaches are to be found in the chronicle literature of the Middle Ages. The clerical chronicler[1] of the early Middle Ages listed; the aristocratic chronicler always narrated. But the clerical chronicler of the High Middle Ages, from about the middle of the twelfth century, was often engaged in explaining the human happenings that came before his eyes.

The writer who proposes to explain human action has a much more difficult task than the writer who attempts to explain nature. Both of them must have some a priori notion of how things happen (the first chapter has shown this to be true for the medieval scientist). But the writer on physical science has, furthermore, a very large body of concrete data already organized for him; as a scientist, he inherits an already shaped world. The medieval scientist (like his modern counterpart) presumed the existence of an inclusive system—in the thirteenth century, the descending

---

1. This chapter depends chiefly upon materials found in two collections, the Rolls Series, *RS,* and *Nelson's Medieval Classics* (vols. unnumbered, London, Thomas Nelson and Sons, 1949–date), hereafter *NMC.* I have made some use of the translations provided in the latter series, but most of the translations are my own. I have translated with painful literalness in most cases in order to preserve the medieval character of the narrative. Most modern translators instinctively push medieval materials toward modern perceptual modes.

forces generated by the primum mobile—and hence every particular explanation was in some sense determined by the shape of the whole system. In order to confirm this character of medieval science, one need only consider Grosseteste's speculations about light.[2] This speculation led to what was, perhaps, the most original scientific theory of the medieval period.[3] Not only did it remain entirely within medieval perceptual modes, it also utilized at every step the concrete premises and data of medieval Aristotelianism, and it took for granted the overall system proposed by the Aristotelianism.

The medieval writer about human affairs had neither the organized body of fact nor the system of the scientist. He had, of course, an a priori conception of how things happen—explanation is impossible without such conceptions—but he had no system into which particular explanations might be fitted. Furthermore, the traditions determining the scope of his account and the manner of relating happenings to each other were loose and vague. In short, every entry in a medieval chronicle involved many more choices than ever confronted the scientist.

Because of these differences, a modern scholar must approach the clerical chronicle of the Middle Ages with circumspection. The presuppositions entering into medieval science might be shown by examining the articulations of the broad system; no such closed system operates in the chronicles.

One consequence of this lack of system is that the material can only be dealt with representatively. There are dozens of medieval chronicles whose modes of perception identify them as clerical, and they very naturally differ in some respects from one another. It is impossible to deal with even a representative portion of these chronicles in detail when close reading is required. The only practical approach is to deal with representative chronicles in some depth and to allow the generalizations which emerge to stand for the whole class. This procedure is possible because the clerical view of action was very narrow. One may hence

2. See especially *De luce seu de inchoatione formarum, Die Philosophischen Werke des Robert Grosseteste,* Resorgt von Dr. Ludwig Baur, Beitrage zur Geschichte der Philosophie des Mittelalters, Texte und Untersuchungen (Munster, Aschendorff, 1912), 9, 51–59.

3. A. C. Crombie, *Robert Grosseteste and the Experimental Origins of Modern Science,* 1100–1700 (Oxford, Oxford University Press, 1953).

describe a norm which is generally valid for the whole class of chronicles, even though individual members of the class may have departed from it in various minor ways.

The medieval clerical chronicle must be approached analytically, in terms of the process which more or less unconsciously resulted in characteristic medieval history writing. The process can be elucidated by seeking answers to three questions: By what principle did the chronicler decide what belonged in his chronicle? How did he understand causation? What shape did he see in the human experience he was engaged in relating?

Relevance and Interest

The most characteristic product, although not the only one, of the medieval clerical chronicler's art is perhaps best described as the "universalizing chronicle." This term must not be taken to imply that some sort of universal history was the chronicler's objective; a universalizing chronicle is simply one which did not self-consciously pursue a single line of action, but moved about freely among a variety of interests. There were a great many such chronicles in the Middle Ages, but the *Chronica majora* of Matthew Paris is generally regarded as the greatest specimen of this type, and it can be taken to stand for them all.

However, one preliminary observation about these universalizing chronicles must be made. They are the obvious descendants of the one-line annual entries of the *Anglo-Saxon Chronicle,* and to casual inspection they read like journals, with entries simply jotted down as things of interest occurred. But this was not how the great majority of such chronicles were written; reference is frequently made to information reported in subsequent entries. So habitual are such references that one of the great editors of these chronicles, Richard Howlett, used them to establish a terminus ad quem for the *Gesta Stephani.* Matthew Paris, of course, reworked his texts very carefully; the different recensions of essentially the same narrative show this to be the case.[4] The shape

4. See Richard Vaughan, *Matthew Paris* (Cambridge, England, Cambridge University Press, 1958), passim, but especially pages 110–12. As for Matthew's habit of anticipating events, one may point to the origins of the quarrel between William of Valence and the city of London of

of these chronicles was not the product of circumstances but of
choice.

The organizing principle was chronology; for Matthew Paris,
as for Roger of Wendover, the fundamental unit of organization
was the year. The entries for each year were heralded by a notice
of the king's Christmas festivities, and the end of each year was
indicated by a brief summary of its outstanding events.

But these chronicles do not attempt a chronological narrative;
indeed, the variety of interests reflected in such chronicles made
chronology the worst possible principle for maintaining narrative
coherence. Here, for example, is the sequence of events recorded
for the beginning of 1251:[5]

> The King was at Winchester at Christmas. Of untimely
> winter thunder.
> A sad prognostic [the aforesaid thunder].
> The King does not distribute festive clothing.
> The accustomed bounty of the King's court is cut short.
> Of a certain precaution taken in the Empire.
> The rising of supporters of Frederick begins to be renewed.
> A disagreement arises between two of the most powerful
> sultans of the Saracens.
> Continuation.
> Note the patience of the King of the French.
> Guy, the brother of the Lord King, arrives ingloriously from
> the Holy Land.
> How the King punished him and his other brothers.
> The Bishop of London swears to support ecclesiastical
> censure, and thus he is absolved.

---

which Matthew remarks, "nevertheless the dregs of evil feeling against
the city was not wholly extinguished, as a following passage will declare
more fully" (RS, 57:5, 644). See also his remark, "the bishop, on hearing
this, declared that the king was about to follow the footsteps of certain
conspirators who had already broken out in a similar audacity in France
(of whom there is a fuller narration on a following page)" (RS, 57:4,
191). Howlett uses the chroniclers' habit of referring to later events as
evidence helping to date the Gesta Stephani. Chronicles of the Reigns of
Stephen, RS, 82:3, xii–xiii.

5. Matthew Paris, Monachi Sancti Albani, Chronica majora, ed.
Henry Luard, RS, 57:5, 198–205.

This apparently haphazard selection of subjects is not peculiar to 1251, nor even to Matthew Paris. It is characteristic of all universalizing chronicles.

The confusion is deepened by the fact that Matthew obviously intended, as Richard Vaughan has pointed out, to write a history of England, even while he included accounts of events in "England, Wales, Scotland, France, Germany, Italy, the Iberian peninsula, Denmark, Norway, and the East."[6] Professor Vaughan suggests that, "it appears probable that Matthew, in the course of writing his *Chronica Majora,* found it hard not to include every item of news which came to hand, and that he was aware of the irrelevance, to English history, of much of his material."[7] This is true. But it is also true that irrelevance—*impertinens* as Matthew often calls it—could not mean in the Middle Ages what it means today, that it could not, in fact, constitute a major criterion for the historian selecting his materials. The mere summary of events for 1251, quoted above, makes it clear that Matthew saw no more causal process in his material, human action, than Albertus saw in nature. But relevance, as we understand it today, depends heavily upon a conception of causal processes. When we say that something is relevant to something else, we ordinarily mean that there is a causal relationship between them. Lacking in great measure this perception of relationships, the medieval chronicler who took his work seriously, as Matthew certainly did, was hard put to know what was relevant and what was not.

As a consequence, relevance was simply not Matthew's major criterion of selection; rather, things to be reported were selected upon what might be called "the principle of interest." Every writer in every age has two sources of reader interest at his disposal because human beings are motivated by two kinds of curiosity. One kind arises from the reader's intuition of relevance to himself, at some level, of what is being recounted. History since the sixteenth century has commanded this sort of curiosity from the educated reader, and the connection between history and reader is a perception of causal process shared by both historian and reader. The other kind comes from the innate and often insatiable human pleasure in the odd and wonderful. Any sequence

6. Vaughan, *Matthew Paris,* pp. 125–26.
7. Ibid., p. 112.

of entries will serve to demonstrate the dominance of this latter principle in the *Chronica.* For the year 1248, for instance, following the usual brief note about the king's Christmas, Matthew describes how Simon de Montfort took the cross with many other nobles. The next item reports the appeal made by the Bishop of Bangor to the Abbot of St. Albans for shelter in his wretchedness. There follow brief notices about the illness of Richard Deward, the arrival of a couple of nobles from southern France, gaping after Henry's money, naturally, and the death of a bishop. We then have an account of how the French king reassumed the cross, essentially a description of a kind of public debate between king and advisers. The lengthy account of the parliament at London which follows takes much the same form; this is followed by a dispute between the bishops of Durham and St. Albans.[8]

We can best understand the choice by regarding Matthew as the center of a circle of light which shades off into darkness. Events notable enough to be visible from the central point in this circle of light appear in the *Chronica majora.* Minor incidents close to Matthew, in the abbey for instance, are worth reporting by mere proximity; incidents across the Channel must be in some way correspondingly more spectacular to attract his attention. The principle in each case is essentially pure interest, and not relevance, at least not direct relevance.

Of course these two kinds of interest and the two kinds of curiosity from which they arise are not mutually exclusive. It would be a mistake to argue that a principle of relevance was not operative in Matthew's chronicle; but it operated only in a general sense, determining the class of happenings most worth reporting, but not selecting events within the class. These were selected on the principle of general interest. Thus relevance made the doings of the English king more interesting than the doings of the French one and the events at St. Albans more interesting than those at another monastery. But pure interest determined what specific events should be recorded.

This can be illustrated by a passage which might seem at first glance to show the opposite, Matthew's rather long account of the Parliament of 1248. Matthew begins his account with a lengthy list of the most important people who responded to the summons,

8. Matthew Paris, *Chronica majora, RS,* 57:5, 1–11.

noting (by the way) a few who did not. There is no suggestion, however, that the substantial response had any particular importance; it was obviously a part of the impressiveness of the occasion. The king's demand for money is briefly reported, and the rest of the entry is a long, rather general account of the grievances of prelate and baron. This, in turn, is followed by a brief entry, characteristic of the *Chronica* (if not of Henry III), in which Henry confesses his sins and vows amendment. The nobles are restrained in their enthusiasm by memories of past confessions, the parliament is postponed, and the king returns to normal. In the words of Matthew,[9]

> The king, in the meantime, either of his own accord, or at the instigation of his courtiers, who did not wish their power to be weakened, became obdurate and more exasperated against his subjects, and took but very little trouble to make any amends to them for the above-mentioned excesses, as he had promised to do.

What significance, what relevance, did Matthew perceive in this parliament? None. Parliaments were interesting in and of themselves, in a way not essentially different from the tournament at Newburgh reported a few pages later. Over and over the king formally demanded money from his greater subjects; over and over they resisted. But there is nothing fundamental, connecting these incidents, at work in Matthew's account.

Furthermore, Matthew Paris and the other universalizing chroniclers were not writing a central narrative that was frequently interrupted; no narrative intention, by modern standards, lingers behind this multitude of separate entries. This can be shown by an examination of two entries leading up to the Barons' Revolt. The first entry reports the Parliament of Oxford in 1258. This is described in some detail: first the gathering of the barons, with their retainers armed, contrary to the usual custom; their demands, centering around King John's Charter; the oath of the king and Prince Edward and the refusal of the Poitevins to take the oath. The subsequent meeting of the barons is reported, and the wavering of some is climaxed by a confrontation between the Earl of

9. Ibid., p. 8.

Montfort and the king's brother, William de Valence. The entry concludes with the flight of the Poitevins to Winchester and the rallying of the barons with their supporters into what would appear to be a full-fledged conspiracy.[10]

This is, of course, the beginning of the Barons' War, led by Simon de Montfort. Hostilities were clearly imminent at the time of this entry and, indeed, this Parliament was a critical event in the development of such hostilities. Matthew Paris' concluding remark to his own account seems, as a consequence, peculiar: "and thus ended the Parliament at Oxford, without any fixed and definite result."

Matthew returned to politics, after a half-dozen entries concerned with other matters, with a report of the departure of the king's uterine brothers from England, an entry worth quoting at some length:[11]

> In the octaves of the Translation of St. Benedict . . . the aforesaid brothers of the king, having said farewell took their departure from England, and certain other Poitevins were with them. . . . These Poitevins having refreshed themselves first at Winchester and afterward in the house of the bishop elect of Winchester in London, namely at Southwark, it was said that many nobles of England were treacherously poisoned there and elsewhere, as afterward the outcome of the thing proved more truly. Who, when they had come to the sea, the nobles who conducted them commended them to Neptune. But when they had come to Boulogne, they wrote to the king of France that they might have a peaceful transit or make a delay in his land, according to the antique liberty and custom of France. . . . But the king of France being

10. Ibid., pp. 695–98.

11. Ibid., pp. 702–03. I have chosen this passage for consideration (in spite of the fact that Matthew died the next year and hence perhaps did not rework this section as thoroughly as earlier sections) because it concerns the most important action of Matthew's life, and information about it must have been widely bruited at the time. There is the further consideration that entries as closely related as those under consideration in the text are very rare in the earlier parts of Matthew's *Chronica* or elsewhere. It is significant that the *Historia anglorum* (3 vols. *RS, 44*), which Matthew wrote from the *Chronica majora,* is a less coherent and connected narrative (by modern standards, of course) than the *Chronica* itself.

exasperated refused, because the French queen put a heavy
charge against these same Poitevins, that they had shamefully scandalized and defamed her sister the queen of England; and the king added that they had been shamefully
driven from England for their crimes. On hearing this,
Henry the son of the count of Leicester, with his father either
uninformed or unwilling, or perhaps conniving, pursuing
them hostilely, suddenly crossed the channel.

The rest of the entry deals at some length with this latter abortive
effort.

Most striking about these entries is their discontinuity. The
second entry, in returning to the conflated action covered by the
first, joins with it in the most superficial way. The "nobles" ac-
companying the Poitevins are apparently the barons of the previous entry, although Matthew does not say so. The Poitevins were
actually going into exile at the insistence of the barons. It is incredible that Matthew did not know this fact, a major element in
the relationship between these two entries. But, amid the sensa-
tional reports of poisonings, it did not seem to him worth reporting. A modern reader will see these two entries as fragmentary
reports on an important sequence of action. But he should realize
at the same time that for Matthew and the other clerical chroniclers, the sequence of action—the fundamental connection between these two entries for the modern historian—did not exist.
It was not a part of their perceptual equipment.

This point surely does not need belaboring. The most casual
scrutiny of any modern journal of medieval studies will show
how much time and effort the modern historian must spend col-
lating medieval chronicles and other materials to work out the
most elementary fragment of his own causal processes—the itiner-
ary of a king on his perambulations, for instance, or the movements
of armies in a war. Another illustration is the notorious carelessness
of medieval chronicles in the matter of dating. Thousands of pages
of modern scholarship have been spent just trying to straighten
out chronology. These efforts are necessary to working a causal explanation. The medieval casualness about dates clearly indicates
that the chroniclers were not concerned about causal processes.
They didn't know they existed.

One should note, too, the criterion of selection operative in these entries by Matthew Paris. The response of the king of France was transient and of no consequence, and the activities of Henry the son of Simon were not heard of again. I know of no modern writer who takes the poisonings seriously, but these reports were interesting and striking. The whole entry constituted, in sum, a notable event, and notable events were what the chronicler chiefly reported. Furthermore, there is no reason to suppose that the earlier entry, the parliament, was selected for inclusion in Matthew's *Chronica* on any other basis than that of intrinsic interest.

Principles of Causation

We can most readily understand the medieval feeling for causation in human history (and in human life) if we begin by considering that almost omnipresent feature of clerical chronicles, the innumerable comets, bloody rains, and so forth that the clerical chronicler reported. The modern historian in his most kindly mood is apt to regard interest in these occurrences as an unfathomable eccentricity of his medieval forebears. Eccentric perhaps they are, but they are not unfathomable, and a brief survey of the range of such phenomena is instructive.

The most important were, of course, astrological phenomena. However, the medieval chronicler was rather oddly selective in his interest in astrology. The theory of the planets and their houses, the heart of astrological doctrine, is reflected in these chronicles only rarely, and then usually as explanations of more immediate and more spectacular celestial phenomena.[12] In astrology, as in other matters, the chronicler was drawn to the unusual.

Naturally, a great deal of attention was paid to comets, since

12. Both Gerald the Welshman ("De principiis instructione liber," Dist. III, ch. vi, in *Geraldi Cambrensis opera, 8,* ed. G. F. Warner, *RS, 21:8,* 242–43) and Roger of Hovedon (*Chronica Magristi Rogeri de Hovedone,* ed. W. Stubbs, *RS, 51:2,* 290) report much perturbation about the astrological predictions for 1185; in a footnote Stubbs refers to other notices. More typical, however, is the entry for the year 1260 in the *Flowers,* formerly ascribed to Matthew of Westminster (*Flores historiarum,* ed. Henry Luard, *RS, 95:2,* 453), in which astrology is related to more immediate cosmological disturbances—thunderstorms, lightning, etc.

they were believed to foretell events of major importance. The standard doctrine of comets, so far as the chroniclers were concerned, is recorded in the *Chronicle of Melrose:*[13]

> A comet is a star which is not always visible, but which appears frequently upon the death of a king, or on the destruction of a kingdom. When it appears with a crown of shining rays, it portends the decease of a king; but if it has streaming hair, and throws it off, as it were, then it betokens the ruin of the country.

Comets were of great interest because they were followed by great consequences. At the same time, there was a certain lack of precision in their "portending," even when it was known that "whither it directs its hair, thither does it direct calamity."[14] At times this uncertainty was relieved by special circumstances. The comet of 1402, reported by Adam of Usk, was perfectly unambiguous in its prediction that the Duke of Milan was about to depart from this world; his coat of arms had been thoughtfully added to the usual celestial phenomena of the time.[15] And the premature aviator Elmer,[16] whose lamentation on the appearance of a comet in 1065 is preserved by William of Malmesbury,[17] was obviously vindicated by the horrid event of 1066. Giraldus Cambrensis was positive that a comet foretold the death of Henry II, but his certainty was not unconnected to his political bias; he was writing a tract to promote the interests of the French claimant to Henry's throne.[18]

---

13. Joseph Stevenson, ed., *Chronica de mailros* (Edinburgh, The Bannatyne Club, 1835), p. 70.

14. Because of the unavailability of the Latin text, I have quoted from the Bohn Library translation by H. T. Riley, *Ingulph's Chronicle of the Abbey of Croyland* (London, Bohn Library, 1854), pp. 137–38.

15. *Chronicon Adae de Usk,* ed. and trans. Sir Edward Maunde Thompson (London, Henry Frowde, 1904), p. 75; trans. p. 143.

16. He has achieved a modest modern reputation by trying to fly off the top of a building with imitation bird's wings. This has been seen as an example of the medieval scientific spirit.

17. William of Malmesbury, *Monachi de gestis regum anglorum,* ed. William Stubbs, Bk. 2; *RS,* 90:1, 276.

18. *De principiis instructione liber,* Dist. III, ch. xxviii, p. 306. The meteor was just the beginning; in the Rolls edition, five pages of horrid signs follow.

But these were exceptional cases. Even comets, provided as they
were with a very specific doctrine of significance, were difficult to
relate to individual human events in most instances. Hence the
chronicler often merely suggested the connection. The writer of
the *Annales Henrici Quarti* connected a comet in 1402 with
bloodshed in Wales and Northumbria "as I think."[19] Perhaps
even more commonly, the connection between the heavenly and
terrestrial was simply implicit in the juxtaposition between the
two. Florence of Worcester's report of a comet in 1097 is a typical
entry:[20]

> A star which is called a comet appeared on the third kalends
> of October for fifteen days. Not a few affirmed that they
> saw at the same time in heaven a sign wonderful and as if
> burning, in the form of a cross. Soon after, a dissension
> having arisen between the king and Archbishop Anselm.

Did the celestial event presage this particular terrestrial one?
Florence was obviously suspicious but not positive. Sir Thomas
Gray was unsure of the connection also when he asserted: "At
which time appeared the star comet; also it was a dear year for
corn, and such a lack of food that the mother ate her son."[21]
Comets could wreak their havoc more deviously; according to
The Brut, a "bemyd sterre" seen in 1341 was followed by[22]

> good chepe, and wonder grete plente of chaffaree, vitaile
> and marchanndice, and þare aȝenes, honger, scrafte, mischif,
> and nede of money, inso much þat a quarter of whete att
> London was suolde for .ii s., and a good fatte oxe at a noble,
> and v. good dowe briddes for j d.

19. *Annales Henrici Quarti, Chronica Monasterii S. Albani,* ed. W. T.
Riley, *RS, 28:3,* 338.
20. Florence of Worcester, *Chronicon ex chronicis,* ed. Benjamin
Thorpe (2 vols. London, English Historical Society, 1847–49), 2, 41.
21. *Scalacronica: by Sir Thomas Gray of Heton, Knight,* ed. Joseph
Stevenson (Edinburgh, The Maitland Club, 1836), p. 147. The *Scalacronica* is essentially an aristocratic chronicle (see Chapter 3); this is one
of the rare notices in such chronicles of astronomical phenomena.
22. *The Brut, or the Chronicle of England,* ed. Friedrich Brie, Early
English Text Society (hereafter *EETS*), no. 136 (London, 1908), p. 292.

But Matthew Paris much increased the range of possible interpretations by noting of a certain comet,[23]

> All seeing that *prodigiale* sign wondered, and did not know what it portended. But one thing, although the corn had been almost wholly suffocated with long-lasting rains, in that same hour the time was suddenly entirely altered into a most pure loveliness, which saved the ripe grain, only just ready for the sickle, and permitted it to be gathered.

In the last analysis, comets were mysterious things. Their general relevance to terrestrial affairs was almost universally acknowledged, but their specific significance was often doubtful indeed.

The same general confusion attended other celestial signs of things to come. Prognostication by thunder, as introduced to Western Europe by the Venerable Bede,[24] seems to have been fairly reliable; at least its consequences were, without exception, dire. Thus, according to Matthew Paris, a rainstorm lasting two months was prognosticated by thunder (among other things).[25] A thunderstorm in December 1258, however, only prognosticated bad things to come in a general fashion.[26] The fact that, "contrary to the nature of winter in our part of the world," thunder and lightning occurred on the day when Stephen landed in England was considered very significant by William of Malmesbury.[27]

Lightning bolts striking church steeples were commonly reported but at times difficult to interpret. A continuator of Florence of Worcester said of one such occurrence that "it was indeed not permitted to have happened except as a wonderful portent for all the sons of holy mother church. For on the morrow of

23. Matthew Paris, *Chronica majora, RS,* 57:3, 566. I have not translated *prodigiale* in the text because, as I point out below (p. 62), I do not know what it meant in the Middle Ages.
24. Lynn Thorndike, *Magic and Experimental Science,* 1, 635–36. The text is to be found in *Patrologiae cursus completus,* Series Latina, ed. J. P. Migne (221 vols. Paris, 1844–64), 90, 609–14.
25. *Chronica majora, RS,* 57:3, 339–40.
26. Ibid., *RS,* 57:5, 724.
27. William of Malmesbury, *Historia novella,* ed. K. R. Potter, *NMC,* p. 15.

St. Lawrence, in the same year," the monastery thus visited was taken apart by the people of Norwich.[28]

One of the most famous eclipses in history occurred when Henry I departed for Normandy. According to the well-known passage in the *Anglo-Saxon Chronicle*,[29]

> In this year King Henry went over the sea at Lammas, and on the second day when he lay asleep in the ship the day darkened over all the land, and the sun became as a three-night-old moon, and stars were about him at midday.
>
> Men became very much astonished and fearful, and said that a great thing should come about hereafter, and so it did. For that same year the king died.

The eclipse of 1140, according to William of Malmesbury, was much less specific in its effects; it merely signified that "the king would not pass that year in his office without loss."[30] Toward the end of the twelfth century, Richard of Devises cautioned that "those whom the toil of the world stirs" denied that there was any significance to eclipses,[31] but chroniclers continued to record them and to attribute to them the same range of effects as they did to comets. Walsingham, *The Brut,* and a continuator of the *Polychronicon* all associated the eclipse of 1357 with the drought of the same year.[32]

There was no system behind all this; any unusual natural event was apt to send the clerical chronicler scurrying around looking for human consequences. Two moons, together with a comet, were seen "in token of" the death of Duke Robert in Henry I's prison.[33]

28. Florence of Worcester, *Chronicon ex chronicis*, 2, 207–08.

29. *Two of the Saxon Chronicles Parallel*, eds. Charles Plummer and John Earle (2 vols. rev. ed. Oxford, Oxford University Press, 1929), *1*, 262–63.

30. William of Malmesbury, *Historia novella*, NMC, p. 43.

31. "Richardus Divisiensis, De rebus gestis Ricardi Primi," in *The Chronicles of the Reigns of Stephen, Henry II, and Richard I, RS*, 82:3, 406.

32. Thomas Walsingham, *The St. Albans' Chronicle*, 1406–1420, ed. V. H. Galbraith (Oxford, Oxford University Press, 1937), p. 69. *Polychronicon Ranulphi Higden*, ed. Churchill Babington, *RS*, 41:8, ch. ii, 523–24. *The Brut*, pp. 313–14. The Walsingham entry is obviously the basic one, the continuator of *The Brut* and the continuator of the *Polychronicon* apparently translating from this source independently.

33. Matthew Paris, *Chronica majora, RS*, 57:2, 132.

Four spurious suns seen in the west were followed by a great slaughter in Wales and conflagrations in Ireland.[34] Four circles around the sun in April and a comet in February may or may not have had something to do with dissensions between King Henry and Robert, Duke of Normandy, in 1104.[35] William of Newburgh reported two suns and said: "Nor was it long after this that, the period of truce which had slightly cheered the harassed people being completed, the bloodthirsty rage of the princes once more broke out."[36] But Roger of Wendover reported an elaborate arrangement of suns with no perceptible consequence except the wonder of the beholders.[37]

A persistent, extraordinary star in 1106, together with some other astronomical phenomena, was noted to be followed by a quarrel between the Emperor of Germany and his son.[38] Other circumstances might make for certainty; a fiery ball sailing over the continent from England indicated its victims with precision by splitting itself on a church tower and falling against the doors of the lords whose ruin it heralded, half against each door.[39] The fact that the Northern Lights (apparently) reddened the horizon on three different occasions, each corresponding roughly to disasters to King Richard, confirmed the association of the heavenly with the terrestrial, although even in this instance the chronicler felt obliged to add, "it is believed."[40]

Heavy storms might be felt to be significant and were frequently reported. Roger of Wendover saw the unusual weather and bad crops of 1192 as foreshadowing the ransoming of Richard; however, a certain brightness in the air was a herald of his arrival home after captivity.[41] A tempest of snow in April, coinciding with the coronation of Henry V, was variously interpreted, "as if he was about to be cold in behavior and sharp in rule and

34. Ibid., *RS*, 57:3, 242.
35. Ibid., *RS*, 57:2, 126.
36. William of Parvi, *Historia rerum anglicarum*, Bk. 5, ch. xxv; *RS*, 82:2, 483.
37. Roger of Wendover, *Liber qui dicitur flores historiarum*, ed. H. O. Coxe (2 vols. London, English Historical Society, 1841–44), *I*, 310–11.
38. Florence of Worcester, *Chronicon ex chronicis*, p. 54.
39. *Chronicon Adae de Usk*, pp. 106–07; trans. pp. 287–88.
40. William of Parvi, *Historia, RS*, 82:1, 401–02.
41. Roger of Wendover, *Flores historiarum, I*, 225–31.

government. But other wise men, more discreetly interpreting this intemperance of the air for the best, said that the king made the snows and coldness of vices in the kingdom to fall and sharp fruits of virtues to emerge."[42] This time the optimists had the best of it, according to the chronicler—a more noteworthy fact than the snowstorm.

And of course there were purely terrestrial phenomena. Bloody fountains noticed by chroniclers signified disaster at certain times and nothing in particular at others.[43] More interesting, if less spectacular, was the behavior of the River Dee as noted by Giraldus Cambrensis and passed on by Higden. It had the peculiar ability to indicate by its changes of current the outcome of the perennial battles between the Welsh and English.[44] Another river, reported by William of Newburgh, indicated future scarcity by its copious flow.[45] A change of course by a certain river indicated the division between King Richard II and the people,[46] and dolphins playing in the Thames prognosticated, "according to some," the tempest which followed a short time thereafter.[47]

Earthquakes, although rare, were also meaningful in human affairs. Of the earthquake of 1081, the Westminster chronicle reported that "it is believed that it happened as a sad presage of the change of decrees, laws, and regulations which took place in the before-mentioned council."[48] Most impressive of all was an earthquake in 1440 which was prognostic of an extensive rising of the Commons in the following year.[49]

---

42. *St. Alban's Chronicle*, p. 69.

43. The spring flowing a whole day with unmixed blood after Llewellyn ap Griffith's head was washed in it smacks of miracle, being reported by a fellow Welshman, Adam of Usk (*Chronicon Adae de Usk*, p. 55; trans. p. 218), but the blood seeping from the ground in Berkshire before the death of William II was pure prodigy, in view of William's villainy. (Henry of Huntingdon, *Historia anglorum*, ed. Thomas Arnold, RS, 74, 232.) Matthew Paris reported the same Berkshire phenomenon without comment: *Chronica majora*, RS, 57:2, 115.

44. *Polychronicon*, RS, 41:2, ch. xlii, 26.

45. William of Parvi, *Historia*, 1, xxxviii; RS, 82:1, 84–85.

46. "Annales Ricardi Secundi," in *St. Alban's Chronicle*, RS, 28:3, 229.

47. *St. Alban's Chronicle*, p. 98.

48. Roger of Wendover, *Flores historiarum*, RS, 95:2, 251–52.

49. *Ingulph's Chronicle of the Abbey of Croyland*, 2nd continuation, p. 412.

Nor did these peculiar connections necessarily run from non-human to human events. Both the writer of the *Annales Henrici Quarti* and Adam of Usk reported a mass gang war among the youths of London in 1400 as a prodigy, the writer of the *Annales* connecting it with an episode of celestial warfare which followed shortly afterward, Adam with the subsequent plague.[50] And of course there were numerous portents at critical moments: the failure of Stephen's candle before a battle,[51] the bat and a bell mysteriously sounding at Richard I's coronation,[52] the loss of a shoe, spur, and finally crown at the coronation of Richard II.[53] The list could be extended indefinitely.

In short, any spectacular natural phenomenon was apt to be interpreted in the Middle Ages as prognostic of some purely human event; indeed, even human events in certain circumstances might be prognostic. This frame of reference made cause and effect, medieval style, a matter of no little wonderment in human affairs. When a comet was followed in a year or so by the death of a king—well, the connection was clear enough; sometimes other relationships helped to establish a connection. A continuator of the *Polychronicon* reported an incident thus illuminated: "This yere were seen thre soones atoones, and anone folowyd the threfolde rule and governaunce in the chirche."[54] In this instance, the familiar doctrine of correspondences illuminated a natural, or unnatural, phenomenon that might have been otherwise inexplicable; the numerical parallel, as well as the sun–church parallel,[55] established the connection satisfactorily. But such

50. *Chronicon Adae de Usk*, p. 45; trans. p. 206; *Annales Henrici Quarti*, p. 332.

51. Henry of Huntingdon, *Historia anglorum*, RS, 74, 271. See also the *Gesta Stephani*, p. 55.

52. *Ricardus Divisiensis, De rebus gestis Ricardi Primi*, p. 384.

53. *Chronicon Adae de Usk*, p. 42; trans. pp. 200–02.

54. *Polychronicon*, RS, 41:8, 563.

55. I would suggest that the amount of this in medieval English literature, and chronicles particularly, has been overrated. When it occurs, as here, it seems frequently to have been regarded as some sort of divine sign. In spite of the great attention paid to parallelism by modern historians (Gilson would have this sort of typology characteristic of the science of the twelfth century: see Etienne Gilson, *La Philosophie au moyen age*, pp. 325–28) my own conviction is that it was felt to be esoteric—literary in the bad sense—in its heyday. It did not operate perceptually—it was frosting of the kind the Middle Ages dearly loved.

correspondences were, alas, uncommon, and the significance of a wonder in nature was consequently often in doubt.

Even the time sequence was apparently not a trustworthy guide. For a natural phenomenon to "portend" or "prognosticate," one would assume that it would invariably precede, at no excessive interval, the human event. But a bloody shower in Anglo-Saxon times, accompanied by a cross on men's clothes, might have prognosticated, according to Henry of Huntingdon, the imminent invasion of the Danes or the fall of Jerusalem several hundred years later.[56] A continuator of Florence of Worcester related some red Northern Lights to bloodshed which had taken place six months earlier in Northumberland and elsewhere, although he felt obliged to add a "perchance."[57] Matthew Paris suggested on several occasions that astrological phenomena were disturbances reflecting precedent turmoils in human affairs.[58] But these were exceptional cases, significant as indicating the general insecurity of attribution.

What was the specific connection between the nonhuman phenomenon (ordinarily) and the subsequent human event, between the sign and consequence? There is no clear-cut answer. It is likely that the chroniclers writing the accounts would have, if pressed, located sign, consequence, and connection between the two in the will of God, and indeed, phenomena parallel to those surveyed here were on occasion so attributed.

But one must keep in mind the distinction proposed in the introduction, between beliefs so basic as to be a part of one's perception and beliefs of a lesser order, the ones which are somehow chosen. There is no doubt that celestial phenomena could be of the first order, perceived as divine signs. But the unmistakable mark of divinity was some clear moral antecedent which merited God's beneficence or—more commonly—His vengeance.[59] Sacri-

56. Henry of Huntingdon, *Historia anglorum*, RS, 74, Bk. 4, p. 128.
57. Florence of Worcester, *Chronicon ex chronicis*, 1st continuation, p. 113.
58. Matthew Paris, *Chronica majora*, RS, 57:5, 503.
59. An unusual amount of celestial disturbance might be regarded as a sign of the imminence of the Last Judgment, of course; see *Chronica majora* for the year 1244: RS, 57:4, 345–46. Adam of Usk also provides a list of the signs of the last judgment, *Chronicon Adae de Usk*, pp. 111 ff.

lege was particularly apt to call forth foreshadowings of God's wrath.

It is equally certain that, on the level of perception, a comet or a prodigy was not necessarily the will of God; this is shown by the fact that theological appeals could be made against them. William the Conqueror's response to bad omens before the battle of Hastings is well known: "committing myself trustfully to my Creator in every matter, I have given no heed to omens."[60]

The relationship between sign and consequence where moral antecedent was lacking seems to have been largely a matter of taste or mood. Some chroniclers, like William of Newburgh and the anonymous author of the *Gesta Stephani,* were much more inclined to see the Divine Hand in events than other writers. Perhaps it did not make much difference. When moral antecedents were lacking (as was commonly the case), these marvelous phenomena made no sense as divine signs, since the events which they proclaimed were almost invariably either totally mysterious, until after the fact, or unavoidable. To attribute them to God when they bore no comprehensible relationship to God as personality or moral agent was not to "explain" them. Hence most of these phenomena were not so attributed, and it is likely that among the rest piety frequently specified the attribution which was not really perceptual. By and large, these marvelous occurrences had no clear antecedents.[61]

At the same time, the signs were not themselves ultimately causal. When connections between astrological and human events

60. *Chronicon monasterii de bello* (London, impensis Societatis, 1846), p. 3 (no editor given).

61. It should be pointed out that providence, in these medieval chronicles, operated in the same way that natural phenomena did, discontinuously. This is most apparent in the very providential chronicle, the *Gesta Stephani.* The author sees providence in the successful invasion of Mattilda, although Stephen was very much the hero of this book; the explanation is that the invasion was in punishment for the sins of England, not of Stephen (pp. 56–57). But it was "a wonderful judgement of God" that a certain Robert was caught up in his own misdeeds (p. 70), and later it was providence that enabled Stephen to capture a castle (p. 121). Providence never illuminates anything in medieval chronicles; as the *Gesta* asserts, "every man is blind and altogether ignorant with regard to God's providence and his judgments" (p. 94). In short, *providentia* is another word, like *natura,* that should never be translated into a modern language.

were specified, they were not described as causes; they were "in sign of," they "prognosticated," or they "foretold." There is no way of knowing what these terms meant to their users; it is manifest that they meant nothing very precise; and many connections were not specified at all—they were implicit in juxaposition. What we are probably dealing with here is the late classical sense of a brooding power behind nature, blind, inscrutable, and habitually malicious, which hung over human affairs. In late classical times this power was commonly embodied as the goddess Fortuna.[62] This lady was of course also well known to the chroniclers; "fortune sported in the mutability of human affairs,"[63] "fortune shewede mutabilitie in victory,"[64] and so forth. But there were analogous principles of explanation. William of Newburgh referred the fall of Sicily to the Emperor of Germany in 1194 "more by the malice of chance than by external violence," and Matthew Paris used a similar expression.[65] But more interesting, if more ambiguous still, are the frequent references to "the world" as some sort of force beyond the human realm.[66]

These dark places in the medieval sense of causation may tell us something about the medieval spirit beyond medieval modes of perception. But they were also inherent in medieval modes of perception, as we shall see.

However we may interpret these very common references to the force of natural powers in human affairs, two conclusions are surely inescapable. The first is negative: the medieval clerical chronicler, like his contemporary medieval scientist, had no sense of the world as interrelated causal processes. Lacking a feeling for the world as interrelated but distinguishable processes, the

62. The classical study is of course that of Howard R. Patch, *The Goddess Fortuna in Medieval Literature* (Cambridge, Mass., Harvard University Press, 1927), which surveys late classical ideas.

63. Matthew Paris, *Chronica majora, RS,* 57:4, 137, "ludente fortuna in mortalium mutabilitate."

64. *Polychronicon, RS,* 41:8, 475.

65. William of Parvi, *Historia, RS,* 82:2, 428: "casus magis malitia quam vi externa expugnatum." Matthew Paris uses a similar expression: "Et dum haec fatalis alea mundi revolvisset," *Chronica majora, RS,* 57:4, 386.

66. It should perhaps be pointed out that even in such medieval commonplaces as the definition of man's enemies as "the world, the flesh, and the devil," "the world" necessarily meant something different than it does today.

clerical chronicler, in his attempt to explain the world and its ways, had too many choices and too few applicable criteria to help him narrow his range.

To perceive the world in terms of causal processes is to limit the kinds of relationships we can see between different events. In our daily lives, as in our laboratories, we approach problems of explanation already knowing the way things happen, the causal processes (or lines of force, as it were) by which the world moves; it is in terms of some particular causal process we assume to be operative in a specific event that we seek the prior events which can provide an appropriate explanation. The exact assumptions entering into such an explanation and the intellective process by which a particular causal process is selected may be obscure, but a selection is obviously made, and this selection is a major limitation upon the range of specific explanations available to us.

An example will perhaps clarify the point. Modern physical and social science, in the usual view, is engaged in testing hypotheses and formulating general laws. But behind particular hypotheses lie assumptions which are not ordinarily testable, and these assumptions have to do with the particular causal process which must be operative in a particular situation. The essence of science, in the modern view its methodologies, can be seen as elaborate ways of isolating causal processes on grounds which must be a priori and which are not scrutinized in an experiment itself. To give a single example: the methodology of behaviorism is so designed (more or less unconsciously) as to make a nonbehavioral answer to a hypothesis impossible at any point. It functions to confine potential laws to the framework of assumptions in which a particular hypothesis is formulated. A behaviorist gives a behavioral account of human activity because his methodology, reflecting his assumptions, makes any other explanation impossible.

The impulse to seek an explanation entirely within a particular causal framework is a general phenomenon in the modern world. For instance, the great majority of modern historians see the events with which they deal as explicable by reference to human motivation, to changing human institutions (economic or political), or to some unspecified combination of the two; they construct histories out of their raw materials with their assumption about the critical nature of a particular causal process always operative. Of course, the methods of history cannot be so rigorously exclusive as those of science, and the causal processes of the historian are never perfect, except in theories of history such as that of Marx. A storm at sea, for instance, might be, unmistakably, a critical event in a nation's history, and storms at sea do not belong to any acceptable historical process. Hence, the normal impulse of an historian confronted with a cataclysm is to reduce it to an accident by seeking antecedent conditions within his particular causal process which might make vulnerability to cataclysms inevitable.[67]

There is no need to be critical of this modern faith in causal processes (although it might be well to cultivate an awareness of them). Principles of selection there must be if the universe is to be intelligible. The medieval chronicler, lacking the modern presumption of regular orders of causation, had no principle by which he might exclude nonhuman phenomena from human affairs. Consequently, human history and human life were habitually interrupted and reversed by nonhuman forces. Sometimes these forces were quite outside nature itself.

If we attempt to understand the significance of these extraordinary happenings in human affairs positively, the connection between the medieval view of nature and the clerical view of human affairs is obvious. Given a red rain, a comet, or juvenile delinquency on a mass scale, the clerical chronicler—and at least a great many educated men, surely—asked, "What does it mean?" In the Middle Ages to ask this question of any sort of event was really to ask to what other event, ordinarily of some human significance, it might be related. The relationship was a direct one, mediated by the same sense of occult causation that pervaded medieval physics. There were no mediating steps, no sequence, no pattern of response. What was the significance of the comet of 1132? The death of King Henry. How? Chroniclers, and presumably most educated men, did not ask the question.[68] The

67. To the nineteenth century, of course, the Spanish Armada seemed, at least in part, a natural cataclysm acting decisively in human affairs—which is why modern history has paid it so much attention.

68. It was of course the function of natural philosophers to ask such questions. For instance, Albertus Magnus attributed the evil effect of comets to prior astrological influences—of Mars, specifically (Meteororum, Bk. 1, tractate 3, ch. xi; OO, 4, cols. 507–08). Such an explanation neither

connection was frequently tentative, of course, because there were no principles of selection to limit attribution. The test that ordinarily determined what human event was connected with the nonhuman was ordinarily commensurability, with pure astonishment the significant quality linking the two events. A spectacular consequence was the necessary sequel to a spectacular natural disturbance: this was the one assumption that the chronicler could safely make.

Of course, only a small proportion of the events catalogued in the medieval chronicles involved these extra-natural phenomena. Even for the chronicler most attentive to comets, bloody fountains, and so forth, the great majority of events that engaged his attention were in the realm of the purely human. Wonders are not for that reason irrelevant to an understanding of the medieval view of human action; they give us insight into the medieval sense of causation. They constitute a bridge between medieval nature and medieval man. The world of nature and the world of man were seen through the same perceptual modes by the chronicler writing in the clerical tradition: the shape of history was the shape of nature.

The Shape of History

The clerical chronicler did not see the materials he recorded as constituting a continuum of action. Every new page of the clerical chronicle was potentially, at least, a new beginning; interest, not relevance, was the criterion determining selection. The clerical chronicler was in every case confronted by an excessively wide choice of causes; he had no modern conception of causality to limit his range. Consequently, he tended to relate happenings upon the basis of commensurability—a big war had a big cause. (Readers familiar with medieval chronicles will recall that incommensurability was habitually treated as an ironic reflection upon man's

---

denies the significance of comets nor particularly contributes to their intelligibility. But it is still astonishing how little the chronicles, which were ordinarily written by well-educated men, reflect any influence from contemporary science. Higden, who drew heavily upon most contemporary scientists in his theoretical sections, absolutely ignored them in his historical accounts and the natural phenomena reported in them.

presumption in attempting to understand anything about the operation of the world, God's province, at all.[69])

But the clerical chronicler not only chose the events with which he proposed to deal, he gave them shape. Or rather, his materials presented themselves to him already possessing shape. What constituted that basic block of information out of which all clerical chronicles are constructed, what I will call an "event"? The answer to this question will involve a brief historical excursus, but first it must be noted that the fully developed clerical chronicle of the thirteenth century consists of not one but two sorts of entries. The simpler of these, which might better be called a "fact-event" than an event, can be illustrated by a brief entry from Matthew Paris' *Chronica:*[70]

> And about the same time, the Lord King, softened by friendly prayers, in that he was a most kindly man and had the good will of all, restored to Roger, the lord bishop of Chester, his barony in friendly peace.

Such an entry has no temporal dimensions because, as reported, it has no consequences, and hence, however much elaborated, it refers to one particular instant in time. It simply happened, and it was interesting enough to merit mention. Its presence in the *Chronica* is perhaps sufficiently explained by the principle of interest.

But it is an entry with a background. It is exactly analogous to hundreds of entries in the *Anglo-Saxon Chronicle,* for instance. An editor of the latter document has suggested that such entries were *memoria technica,* mere stimulants to the fully memorized history.[71] Perhaps this was the case with the early entries in the *Anglo-Saxon Chronicle.* But one needs to note also that the most obvious characteristic of such entries, the lack of temporal dimension, generally marks chronicle-writing in England from the eighth to the middle of the twelfth century. Here is a characteristic pas-

---

69. See Henry of Huntingdon's exclamation on the accidental death of the heir to the kingdom of France, Philip, in 1129: "Ecce res insolita et admiratione dignissima! Ecce quanta celsitudo, quam cito, quam leviter adnihilata est!" *Historia anglorum, RS,* 74, Bk. 7, p. 252.

70. Matthew Paris, *Chronica majora, RS,* 57:4, 552.

71. *Two of the Saxon Chronicles Parallel,* 2, xix.

sage from the later books of the *Ecclesiastical History* of the Venerable Bede:[72]

> And Theodore came to his church the second year after his consecration, on the 27th day of May, a Sunday, and he continued in it twenty-one years, three months and six days. And soon, having travelled over the whole island, wherever the peoples of the English dwelled, because he was received and heard by all, he disseminated the right order of living and the canonical rite of celebrating Easter, with Hadrian accompanying and cooperating with him in all things. And he was the first among the archbishops to whom all the English churches consented to give their hands. And because both were copiously learned in both sacred and secular letters, as we have said, with a crowd of students brought together, streams of wholesome knowledge poured forth daily to water their hearts, so that they poured forth for their listeners the knowledge of the metrical art, of astronomy and ecclesiastical arithmetic, as well as books of the utmost in sacred literature.

The significance of this passage is apparent when compared to another passage from Bede, this time an early one obviously dependent upon an earlier document:[73]

> This Alban being a pagan to this point, when the commandments of faithless princes raged against Christians, received into his hospitality a certain clerk flying persecutors, whom when he saw to be diligent in continuous prayers and vigils night and day, suddenly being drawn by divine grace he began to emulate his example of faith and piety, and having been taught little by little by his wholesome exhortations, with the shadows of idolatry left behind, he became a Christian with his whole heart. And when he had entertained the aforesaid clerk for a certain number of days, it came to the ears of the wicked prince that the confessor of Christ, for whom the place of martyrdom had not yet been appointed, was hidden in the house of Alban. Whence he

72. The Venerable Bede, *The Ecclesiastical History of the English People,* Bk. 4, ch. ii. *Baedae opera historica,* ed. J. E. King (2 vols. London, Loeb Classical Library, 1930), *2,* 10.

73. Ibid., 1, vii; *1,* 34–36.

immediately ordered his soldiers to search for him very carefully. Who when they had come to the hut of the martyr presented himself to the soldiers for his guest and teacher, in his garment, that is, the hooded cloak with which he was dressed, and he was led in chains to the judge.

And it happened that the judge, at that time when Alban was led to him, stood by the altars to offer sacrifices to demons. And when he saw Alban, immediately having become exceedingly wrathful because he dared to put himself in danger and to offer himself to soldiers in place of the guest he had received, ordered him to be dragged to the likenesses of devils by which he stood.

The second passage has a sequential character absent from the first. It is truly a story, although a story without any dimensions to it beyond the linear one because it proposes simply to relate what happened. There are a good many similar passages in Bede, particularly in the earlier sections of the *History,* and this mode of writing persisted throughout the Middle Ages chiefly in its saints' lives.[74]

The first passage, on the contrary, is static; Bede's impulse in his own narrative is to break it up and to stop its temporal movement. (The first two sentences of the second passage, very probably by Bede himself, show the same impulse.) His impulse is to write a series of fact-events similar to that quoted from Paris' *Chronica.*

This sort of entry shape is characteristic of all clerical chronicles well into the twelfth century (aside from William of Malmesbury, the first chronicler whom I have found to advance beyond such

74. This narrative structure, which seems to me late classical in origin, is very difficult to characterize. It is neither a modern narrative, searching for meaning within experience, nor a value-charged aristocratic narrative (see Chapter 3). It seems to me a narrative which exists for its own sake, but it often manifests a peculiar sidewise movement, a kind of chronic indirection, which can be surrealistic in effect. This style persisted far into the Middle Ages; it is the style of William of Malmesbury, for instance, and it is preeminently the style of later hagiography. It should be noted that Charles V. Jones long ago called attention to the presence of hagiographic and annalistic elements in the work of Bede, and to sharp stylistic differences in the *Ecclesiastical History* as a consequence. "Bede as Early Medieval Historian," *Medievalia et Humanistica,* 4 (1945), 26–36.

elaborated statements is William of Newburgh[75]). It continues as a mark of the clerical chronicle from then on, in varying proportions. The *Eulogium historiarum* of the fifteenth century is almost entirely made up of such entries.[76]

A great many fact-entries were chosen by virtue of something more than interest; they are the product of a way of seeing experience, of a perceptual mode. The elaborated human facts are exactly analogous to the entries in Isidore's *Etymologies,* as described in the first chapter. Indeed, the *De natura rerum* of the Venerable Bede himself is composed of such fact-entries,[77] and medieval theology prior to the eleventh century proceeded in a manner quite parallel to this.[78] When the same organizational pattern appears in widely different materials at roughly the same time, we are surely justified in assuming that their writers have in common something very fundamental—a mode of perception.

But the most persuasive evidence for the perceptual origin of such fact-entries in early chronicles is that the static quality which is their most outstanding trait continues to characterize later chronicle writing, in which the triadal event mentioned earlier is dominant. The perceptual origins of this second kind of event (which first appears, as I have suggested, in the writing of William of Newburgh) are unmistakable.

Here are two entries for the year 1254, and drawn from the *Chronica majora,* which will serve to illustrate this second form of the medieval event:[79]

> In this same year, about the feast of the Purification of the Blessed Mary, Gaston de Bearn, having brought together a multitude of the enemies of the king, rashly attempted to enter, seditiously and with hostility, the city of Bayonne, and

75. See, for instance, Bk. 2, ch. xvi, of the *Historia* (*RS, 82:1,* 139–40), a passage which is unmistakably organized as an event, as described below.

76. *Eulogium* (*historiarum sive temporis*), ed. Frank Hayden, *RS, 9:3,* 333–421.

77. *Venerabilis Bedae opera quae supersunt omnia,* ed. J. A. Giles (London, Whittaker, 1843), 6, 99–122.

78. See J. de Ghellinck, *Le mouvement théologique du XIIe siècle* (2nd ed. Bruges, Desclée de Brouwer, 1948), pp. 1–90, for a general confirmation of this view of early medieval thought, although Father Ghellinck, of course, is not after the structure of thought this present chapter is concerned to delineate.

79. *Chronica majora, RS, 57:5,* 426–27.

to seize it for himself. And Bayonne is a rich city, situated on the sea, second in all Gascony, with a port and ships, and it is strengthened by men of war and especially by the best wine merchants. But most of the citizens hated the king for the many injuries inflicted by him in England. Whence when the city was exposed to danger, with some of the enemy admitted, those entering were seized by those faithful to the king, by means of the lower class of citizens who loved the king, and many of them, who had thus entered as traitors, were punished according to their merits.

The second entry concerns the grief of King Louis after his return to France, occasioned by his capture by the Saracens and the collapse of his crusade. The grief is described, and then Matthew reports:[80]

Finally a certain holy and discreet bishop, consoling him, said, "Beware, my lord and dearest king, that you do not cast yourself into too great a weariness with life and sorrow, which is absorptive of spiritual joy and the stepmother of souls. For it is a great and incalculable sin, because it brings about prejudice to the Holy Spirit. And lead back before the eyes of your reflection the patience of Job, the endurance of Eustace." And he told fully the story of both, how the Lord had regard to both in the end. To this the king replied [that by his sins the church universal was disgraced] . . . Finally a mass in honor of the Holy Spirit was chanted, so that the king might receive the consolation of Him who is above all things. And thereupon he, through the grace of God, accepted the counsels of healthful consolation.

The static quality of both entries, which clearly relates them to the first entry quoted from Bede, is obvious. Both have an air of finality about them because they present their respective actions as though they were self-contained. But there is also something else going on, a kind of interior movement reflecting the passage of time within the limits of the particular entry.

This second form of the event might be described as a disturbance to a preexisting ground working its way to a conclusion. The

80. Ibid., 465–66.

focus of interest is ordinarily, as in the first passage, upon the disturbance, and the focus very often, as here, blurs the temporal structure. But this sort of event always presumes at least three elements: a preexisting situation, an intrusive disturbance, and a consequence. These elements can be easily identified in thousands of entries in clerical chronicles. In the first entry quoted above, the disturbance, the will of Gaston, is presented first. Then we are given the ground against which the disturbance is directed, the city of Bayonne. But then, because he has disordered the elements, Matthew must restate the disturbance, the admittance of some enemy. The consequence of the piece of action is of course the defeat of the conspiracy.

The significance of the shape of this entry can be seen most clearly if we compare it to an hypothetical modern treatment. A modern writer would consider the activities of Gaston as arising from a context of English–Gascon relations. Matthew does not treat it in this way; the activities of Gaston are an intrusion upon the state of Bayonne. Given this radical difference in perception, which means that a modern writer wouldn't have written this particular entry at all, other oddities in Matthew's treatment remain to be accounted for. At some point, a modern writer would have set up an analysis of the political complexion of the city. Matthew separates the citizens from the lower orders because he sees the situation in terms of action and reaction. The citizens are absorbed into the disturbance of Gaston; the lower orders are part of the successful conclusion.

In the second entry we begin with an essentially "unnatural" situation, the grief of the king. The disturbance in the situation is the admonitions of the bishop, dramatized by the king's response; the king's restoration is the consequence.

But perhaps a further illustration will be helpful. Here is a lengthy section of physical action, especially interesting because the clerical mode of perception was singularly ill-suited to handle action of this sort:[81]

> In the same year, when the Count de la Marche, who had always appeared to be the most powerful among all the Poitevins by much, refused to do homage and allegiance to

81. Ibid., *RS*, 57:4, 178–79.

Amphulse, brother of the French king, who had unjustly usurped the county of Poictou by the gift of his brother the king, he, being enraged, began to kick up his heels and repent of what he had undertaken. Then the same Count de la Marche was called peacefully to breakfast with the said Count Amphulse of Poictou, to rejoice in the Christmas season. But on a certain night about four days before Christmas, when he was about to come the next day to do homage according to his promise, having entered into counsel with his wife Isabella that he should, with changed intention, resist violently, he came before Amphulse and said shamelessly to him: "Being deceived and beset, I proposed to do homage to you. But now, my mind being changed, I swear to you and assure you most resolutely, that I will never make nor observe any compact of allegiance with you, injurious man, who have shamelessly taken away his county from my stepson Count Richard, while he was faithfully fighting for God in the Holy Land and wisely and compassionately liberating our captives, thus paying back evil for good." And swelling up with great threats, surrounded by a troop of armed men, with his wife, while the Poitevins bent their bows, he boldly burst through the middle of them, and having set fire to the house in which he dwelt, he suddenly mounted a great horse and fled. By which deed he astonished and enraged the said Amphulse and all those seeing and hearing about this, and he kindled them to vengeance.

This translation is of course painfully and almost unintelligibly literal in order to show how Matthew pulls his materials together into the perceptual shape. The first sentence sets up the ground of the action; the "when" and "then" clauses, the two "who" clauses, and the participial phrase are used to organize a collection of very different facts. The center of the passage is the long second sentence, the action, which is amplified by the third sentence. The last sentence is the simple conclusion to the action, which in the subsequent passage becomes the ground for new action. One can see very clearly in such a passage how Matthew used subordination to organize the flow of experience into a three-stage pattern of his perception.

Nothing could be further from post-Renaissance perceptual modes. For the modern historian, for instance, the beginning of every book is almost entirely arbitrary. To illustrate by the nearest example, the present study: nothing except the book itself begins with Isidore. A longer book might have begun with Pliny, with no loss of coherence, or even with Aristotle. Nor does the modern historian conceive of the stuff of his narrative as arbitrary, foreign intrusions onto a static ground. Modern histories describe processes, the continuous interaction in time of many forces. Lastly, there never is in modern thought the sort of definitive end to action that English clerks in the Middle Ages envisaged. An incident—a world war, for instance—ends, but it was only a manifestation of more important social forces, which continue.

The relationship between the clerical view of human action and the view of nature outlined in the first chapter (which was also, of course, clerical) is manifest. A planet in the ascendancy was a cause; its human consequence was its effect. It was succeeded by another planet in the ascendancy, having another, equally definite, effect. Human events fell into the same pattern. Human events might be likened, even more pertinently, to comets as described in an earlier section of the present chapter, because they presumed a normal precomet situation to which the comet acted as the disturbance. In the human world, the initiating disturbance was ordinarily human will, or, even more strikingly, bare human action, unrelated to considerations of intention. This human will or human action was not seen as an element in an existing situation; it arose against, and not out of, the preexistent ground. The structure of the human-caused and comet-caused events was entirely analogous.

At this point we can understand the medieval habit of attributing some kind of causal force to fortune, the revolving year, the world, and so forth. Action, in the clerical view, did not originate in the precedent situation; it acted as a disturbance to that situation, originating, in some peculiar way, outside it. Consequently such action was perceived to be caused in a much more definite and limited way than is the case in modern thought, even though the range of causal agents was much greater. Modern thought tends to see the cause of an action as the whole precedent situation: World War II was caused by Hitler, interwar monetary policies,

English pacifist sentiment between the wars—the list is endless. Ordinarily, in the clerical view of things, the cause of an action could be identified with a particular human character or human ambition or, at least, human action. But where it could not, there was a strong impulse to posit fortune or whatever as a comparable agent. A pious writer could, of course, substitute for this vague causal agent God Himself. But one or the other, the hand of God or the inscrutable, personified, working of fortune, was inherent in the clerical perception of action.

However, most entries in most clerical chronicles do not achieve the status of full-fledged events; they fall somewhere between the explicitly three-element shape of the ideal event and the simpler fact. They ordinarily fail to achieve the status of an event because the resolution, the definitive conclusion to the action, was either tentative or lacking entirely. Hence the peculiar observation of Matthew Paris about the Parliament of 1258, noted above, that it ended "without any fixed and definite result." It was a parliament with the greatest consequences, as Matthew's own information implied. But Matthew was not looking for consequences, he was looking for the resolution of an action. Alas, he seldom found it.

Of course, reality did not inevitably present itself to the clerical chronicler as an endless succession of events, existing in splendid isolation from each other; events were frequently interrelated. But they did not, for that reason, lose their event-character. An example of this interrelation of events can be found in the *Chronica majora* under the year 1250.[82]

This series of entries begins by reporting the death of William, Bishop of Winchester. Most such entries are simple fact-statements, of course, but in this case Matthew sets up the state of the bishopric as a kind of ground for this action, which does not, however, have any conclusion. The next entry begins, "When the lord king heard of this," a transitional clause which clearly sets up the death of the bishop as the ground for a new action. The king's most eloquent clerks were sent to persuade the monks of Winchester to elect as their bishop the king's brother Ailmar. But the result of this action was inconclusive. Hence we have a second action,

82. Ibid., *RS*, 57:5, 178–83.

parallel to the first and having the same ground, the death of the bishop; the king comes in person to preach the monks a sermon on the advantages of getting along with him. (If Henry III were half as autocratic as this sermon makes him out to be, then indeed all of Matthew's complaints were understatements.) The next section begins, "The monks, in this narrow strait, conferring diligently on these things . . ." The "narrow strait" is obviously the consequence of the king's sermon, and preceding action, as well as the ground for the new action, the debate of the monks. The conclusion of the monks' debates, acquiescence, is the conclusion of the whole section as well.

That Matthew saw the connections in these longer passages in this way is shown by the shape of the individual sections. Here, for instance, is the beginning of the section describing the king's response to the bishop's death:[83]

> When the lord king had heard of this, uttering joyous and brief complaints with dry tears, he immediately tried, with every force which he had available, that his brother Ailmar, although deficient in order, age, and knowledge, should be substituted in that place. He therefore sent at once two of his special clerks, whom he knew to be most wise for every hint, to Winchester with his letters, that by piling up blandishments, threats, and promises they should incline to this the minds of the monks of the cathedral church, to whom the election pertained, that they should demand this same Ailmar as their bishop and pastor of their souls. And those whom he sent for this were John Maunsell and Peter Chacepork, clerks, who employed the greatest diligence that they might bring about the desire of the king, and they enervated the hearts of very many monks, so that they demanded the same Ailmar as guardian—*demanded,* I say, because he was wholly inadequate and unsuitable for the superintending height.

We have here the ground as initial clause, a participial phrase which subordinates the king's feelings to the action, the "he tried." The rest is elaboration of that action. This is the charac-

83. Ibid., 179–80.

teristic structure of the clerical chronicle: situation, action much elaborated, and a conclusion which is brief or perhaps even lacking entirely. The almost invariable elaboration of the action in the event chops up what is being described into clearly demarcated constituent elements, even when several events are strung together.

It might be objected that the *Chronica* is a good deal more consistent in its interests than this analysis suggests, and in a certain way it is more consistent than its modes of perception might allow. But it is not by modes of perception that the *Chronica* transcends its duller brethren. Matthew's emotions unify his book; his malevolence toward Henry III and Pope Innocent provides a central concern to which the chronicle always returns. But these personages do not provide him with continuous action to be followed; they function by habitually triggering actions of enormous interest but with no essential continuity—rather like exceptionally long-lived comets, setting off reaction after reaction (almost all of which Matthew deplored). These actions and reactions make the *Chronica* an interesting book today, but they were connected only through the characters of the agents in which they originated. The things that make these struggles intelligible for the modern reader—the church–state controversy, for instance —were invisible to Matthew.

Modes of Perception in the Occasional Chronicle

Let me repeat: the peculiar shape that entries take in the universalizing chronicles is neither a superficial nor a fortuitous characteristic; it is not a product of the impossible task of dealing with an unlimited subject matter. This shape was imposed by unconscious perceptual organization upon observed experience and was prior to the reporting of it. The proof of this fact is that the clerical chronicler broke up his materials in a very similar way when he was not writing a universalizing chronicle—when he was presenting the elements of what a modern historian would regard as a single line of action. A good example of this sort of work, called an occasional chronicle to distinguish it from the universalizing chronicle, is the *Gesta Stephani,* which illustrates the clerical chronicler's approach to a single line of action. It is especially useful because it does not contain the sort of "fact-event" that litters the universalizing chronicles and might be regarded as in part responsible for the incoherence.

The perceptual world of the universalizing chronicle is manifest in the very beginning of the *Gesta Stephani:*[84]

> When King Henry, the peace of his country and father of his people, came to his last moments and paid his debt to death, the grievous calamity made the entire aspect of the kingdom troubled and utterly disordered. For where, during his reign, had been the fount of righteous judgment and the abode of law, there, on his decease, grew up abundance of iniquity and a seed plot of all manner of wickedness; insomuch as England, formerly the seat of justice, the habitation of peace, the height of piety, the mirror of religion, became thereafter a home of frowardness, a haunt of strife, a training ground of disorder and a teacher of every kind of rebellion.

The balance of the section is an account of the devastation. What we have here, obviously, is the familiar static ground, England at peace, troubled by the decease of Henry I, and disorder as the consequence; the shape is only slightly blurred by the fact that the preexisting ground is presented as the first member in successive contrasts (the fount of righteous judgment, the seat of justice, etc.). Particularly noticeable is the failure of the author to see any sort of connection between the precedent ground, England at peace, and the conclusion, England devastated, except the action, the death of King Henry.

Section upon section thereafter is built on this sort of event pattern. The whole description of Stephen's Welsh activities, gathered at the beginning of the narrative, falls obviously within the pattern.[85] We have at the beginning the peaceful land (this time Wales), the precipitating action of the death of Henry, and the rising of the Welsh as the consequence. This consequence becomes the ground of a new event, with an invasion of English archers constituting its action, and their defeat its consequence. We then embark upon a new sequence: Richard Fitz Gilbert leads

84. *Gesta Stephani,* p. 1.
85. Ibid., pp. 9–14.

troops against Stephen for a ground and is fortuitously defeated and killed by the Welsh; the conquest of his Welsh lands by the latter forms the consequence. This in turn leads to the besieging of Richard's widow by the Welsh and consequently her rescue by "a certain Miles." With the disturbance of Wales again constituting the ground, we have the expedition of Baldwin against them as action, with this event trailing off into the nonconsequential consequence so familiar in accounts of medieval siege warfare. The last of these Welsh entries follows the same pattern, complicated by an action–reaction middle element.

The basic perceptual structure of the *Gesta Stephani,* then, is the same as that of the *Chronica majora;* in a majority of the entries, the simple form is immediately apparent. But there are inevitable differences between the *Gesta* and the *Chronica,* since the author of the *Gesta* limited his subject matter. In the *Gesta,* one is much more apt to find several actions arising successively from the same ground. For instance, the second section, following the opening already described, begins,[86] "Meanwhile, when the English were conducting themselves in so disorderly a fashion and, loosening the restraints of justice, were freely indulging in every sort of impiety, Stephen Count of Boulogne." "Meanwhile" (*interea*), here as elsewhere in clerical chronicles, signals the imminence of a second action arising against the same ground as for the first action—the *Gesta* has a good many meanwhiles.

Furthermore, because the author has at least a rough principle of selection, the deeds of Stephen, he has a great many more chains of action–reaction than Matthew, and they are apt to be more complicated. The landing of Robert Earl of Gloucester and his sister Matilda touches off a very complicated series of events.[87] The initial ground was Stephen's preoccupation elsewhere; the action was the landing; the consequence was general alarm among the population. But Stephen's courage turns the landing into the ground for a new action, the investing of the castle where they had landed. The outcome was inconclusive. Then two actions on the part of the Bishop of Winchester follow against the same ground, the landing. The first action was the blockade of the area, and this led (according to rumor) to a pact with Earl Robert.

86. Ibid., p. 2.
87. Ibid., pp. 58–60.

The second action was an argument with Stephen about the value of the siege; its lifting was the consequence. The lifting of the siege, as a new ground, led to the recruiting activities of the countess as the action, with the defection of many from their allegiance to Stephen the consequence.

This is obviously a complicated section, but the complexity is not the result of a new perceptual mode. It remains the event as it is found in medieval physics: the collision between a ground and an action essentially foreign to it leading to a new situation.

This account covers a large proportion of the *Gesta Stephani* (about seven-eighths). The few passages which lie outside this account are fragments reflecting the second major medieval perceptual category, the aristocratic. It will be convenient to postpone consideration of these modes in the *Gesta* until we turn to this second category.

The English chronicler of the Middle Ages did not see in human experience the causal processes fundamental to modern experience. He saw human action as he saw natural action, as an endless series of events, frequently related but at the same time possessing a unique structure that kept them discrete. His experience of the human world was, consequently, not comparable to ours.

Action and change in this medieval view were not implicit and natural to human existence and institutions. The natural and normal state was always the preexistent ground; action was a disturbance of the norm, an unnatural state of affairs. This fundamental attitude toward experience was responsible for the pessimism which modern scholarship has recognized as an omnipresent attitude in clerical chronicles. The chronicler was mostly engaged in reporting events which should not have happened, since the ideal and presumably "normal" state of affairs was one which would have precluded the very subject matter of the chronicle.

Such a statement of course needs some qualification. Some entries in medieval chronicles give approval to what is recorded. For instance, Matthew Paris was entirely in favor of the efforts of the barons to organize against Henry. But he did not regard the barons as initiating anything. Henry III was the great initiator from Matthew's point of view; the barons were seen as reacting, bent upon expelling the disturbance to quiescence—the wicked, foreign counselors of the king. The very shape of individual entries frequently reflects this point of view.

In addition, this view of action as a disturbance of a norm which was necessarily nonaction was constantly in conflict with an almost universal ethical imperative of the period—the necessity, borrowed from the aristocratic mode of perception, to enlarge one's personal estate, one's monastery, one's kingdom. This imperative obviously compelled men to make disturbances out of themselves by self-aggrandizement, while at the same time they posited quiescence as the proper condition for the rest of the universe. But this is only to say that there was a basic incoherence in the medieval world-view, and it was an incoherence more or less invisible to medieval men, since the incompatible forms of behavior were so readily apportioned. For Matthew Paris, the obligation of his monastery, St. Albans, to expand its privileges and possessions— to disturb the existing order, in fact—was self-evident. Equally self-evident was the obligation of king and pope to maintain the old relationships, the status quo—St. Albans excepted. Perhaps King Henry III and Pope Innocent felt much the same way about it, envisaging only a slight rearrangement of roles. All parties heartily agreed, in theory, that disturbance was a bad thing. There should be no mystery about this sort of paradoxical conservatism to the twentieth-century student of the Middle Ages; it did not end in 1500.

These qualifications are not important to the main point, that the medieval clerical chronicler, confronted by a sequence of action to record, saw it through the same sort of perceptual categories that conditioned his view of nature. He saw—and he had no choice in the matter, even though the mode of seeing had been taught him—an aggregate of more or less discrete units of action, which we may call events. For these events to have meaning and be understood, they were necessarily organized into triads: a ground, an intrusive action, and a consequence.

CHAPTER 3

Perception of Human Action: The Aristocratic Chronicles

Compared with the number of clerical chronicles, few aristocratic chronicles are to be found in medieval England; they are typically written in Old French or one of its variants. For this study I have chiefly drawn upon the *Chronique de la guerre entre les Anglois et les Ecossois* of Jordan of Fantosme, dated 1174, the *Histoire de Guillaume le Marechal,* dated about 1226, the *Chronicle* of Pierre de Langtoft, dated 1307, and, for the fourteenth century, the *Scalacronica* of Sir Thomas Gray and the *Life of the Black Prince* by the herald of Sir John Chandos. To this list of English sources I have added the *Chroniques* of Sir John Froissart. The *Chroniques* are indispensable to an understanding of medieval aristocratic thought. Most aristocratic writers assume aristocratic stances even while they write about them; they do not notice things that do not cohere within those stances. Sir John was an aristocrat in his modes of perception as in his allegiances, but he lived in the aristocratic world not by right but by tolerance, for his role was that of a chronicler of aristocratic activities, not an aristocrat. As a consequence, he tells us things the average chronicler would not notice.

The above list is not, of course, exhaustive,[1] nor were all aristo-

---

1. In addition to the chronicles listed above, I have consulted G. H. Orpen, ed. and trans., *The Song of Dermot and the Earl* (Oxford, Oxford University Press, 1892); *L'Estorie des engles solum la translacion maistre Geffrei Gaimar,* ed. T. D. Hardy and C. T. Martin, *RS, 91;* Ambroise, *L'Estoire de la guerre sainte,* translated as *The History of the Holy War* by Edward Stone, in *Three Old French Chronicles of the Crusades,* University

cratic chronicles, as defined in this chapter, invariably written in French. The Middle English *Chronicle* of Robert of Gloucester is clearly aristocratic in its later sections,[2] as is, by and large, the Latin chronicle of that twelfth-century wonder, Geoffrey of Monmouth.[3] But the advantage in defining the aristocratic mode of perception by reference to the above-mentioned Old French or Anglo-Norman exemplars is that the language itself provides reasonable assurance of their aristocratic orientation.

The superficial, identifying characteristics of these chronicles can be readily enumerated. They are concerned only with the knightly class, and they are concerned with that class as heroes of council and field (although domestic and ceremonial matters are noticed). As a consequence, a fourteenth-century king and his barons are frequently described as though they were a war band left over from *Beowulf*. In the second place, these chronicles are strikingly bare of the explanatory cosmology—the references to comets, to fortune, and so forth—that characterize clerical chronicles. Even references to God are comparatively rare and casual, and their function, when they occur, is very apt to be rhetorical rather than explanatory, as in the following passage from Jordan of Fantosme:[4]

---

of Washington Publications in the Social Sciences, 10 (Seattle, University of Washington Press, 1939); *The Crusade and Death of Richard I,* ed. R. C. Johnston, Anglo-Norman Texts, 17 (Oxford, Blackwell, 1961); *Master Wace, the Chronicle of the Norman Conquest from the Roman de Rou,* trans. Edgar Taylor (London, Pickering, 1837). As the above list indicates, aristocratic chronicles by Englishmen, or closely associated with England, are chiefly found in the twelfth century. Since such chronicles were in a very bad position to survive, this is perhaps an historical accident.

Of the chronicles listed above, the *Crusade and Death of Richard I* seems to me a mindless sort of compilation from other sources. The others belong to what seems to be the "pure" aristocratic tradition, exemplified in the following study chiefly by the *Life of the Black Prince,* and hence their inclusion in the study, except incidentally, would contribute little to its conclusions.

2. *The Metrical Chronicle of Robert of Gloucester,* ed. William A. Wright, *RS, 86,* Parts I and II.

3. *The Historia Regum Britanniae of Geoffrey of Monmouth,* ed. Acton Griscom (London, Longmans, Green, and Co., 1929).

4. *Chronique de la guerre entre les Anglois et les Ecossois en 1173 et 1174, par Jordan Fantosme,* ll. 84–91, ed. Richard Howlett, *Chronicles*

He [Henry II] drew up his baronage with a fierce countenance;
He goes against Louis, the rich king of France,
Against the Count Philip, of whom you hear talk,
And Lord Matthew his brother, a knight of valor.
God aided the father much that day, when He helped him,
And He showed a fair omen about his war;
For the helper of his son, in whom the son's hope most was,
Was this day overthrown without delay.

This rhetorical reference to God is clearly a part of the amplification designed to lend dignity to the events described.

There are, of course, exceptions to this characterization. Froissart has passages prodigious in nature,[5] references to God which are explanatory,[6] and other classes are occasionally noted. Nor are these chronicles absolutely uniform. *The Life of the Black Prince,* written by that most aristocratic of functionaries, a herald, might be regarded as a "pure" aristocratic chronicle; on the other end of the scale, the *Chronicle* of Pierre de Langtoft, as well as the *Scalacronica,* show some clerical influence, no doubt because their authors had enough clerical education to ransack Latin chronicles for the earlier parts of their account. But taken altogether and compared to the clerical chronicles, these narratives do constitute a distinct genus.

We can get at the essential characteristics of the aristocratic chronicle by an examination of two fairly long quotations. The first comes from the twelfth-century chronicle of Jordan:[7]

---

of the Reigns of Stephen, Henry II, and Richard I, RS, 82:3, 210. The Rolls Series editors of Old French texts ordinarily provided a translation along with the text, and I have of course made use of these. However, any modern translator will tend to modernize his text by removing or blurring just those characteristics of the original of particular interest in this study. I have hence taken the liberty of proposing my own translations, even at the risk of falling into egregious error.

5. Sir John Froissart, *Chroniques de France, d'Engleterre, d'Escoce,* etc., in M. le baron Kervyn de Lettenhove, ed., *Oeuvres* (25 vols. Brussels, V. Devaux, 1867–77), *5,* 48–49; *14,* 234–35.

6. *The Chronicle of Pierre de Langtoft,* ed. Thomas Wright, *RS, 47:2,* 29–31, 37–39, 227–29 (lines are not numbered in the text).

7. Jordan, *Chronique,* ll. 339–62; *2,* 232–34.

When the king of England hears the ultimatum
Of his cousin of Scotland, of his intention,
He says to his messenger that he will by no means do it;
He seeks not to have at call either stranger or kinsman.
"Say to the king of Scotland that I am not terrified
"By the war that I happen to have with my son at present,
"Nor by the king of France, nor by his people,
"Nor by the count of Flanders, who frequently attacks me.
"I will make them wrathful and sorry for their war,
"And I will pay him back, if God permit.
"But tell his brother, David, my relation, on my behalf,
"That he should come to help me with as many men
            as he has.
"I will give him so much land and so many fiefs,
"I will perform all his requests according to his desire."
   "Sire," says the messenger, "I promise it to you;
"But give us leave to go in safety."
Then the messengers have departed from Normandy,
They find a good passage across, and make no delay there.
They cross to England, they come to Albany.
The messengers are wise, they care not for folly:
They meet with no one who molests them or speaks
            evil to them
From the Sea of Dover as far as Orkney.
Now they tell such a message of war through a dispute
At which those who have heard nothing of it shall weep.

The second passage is from Froissart:[8]

A short time after the Bishop of Lincoln had returned to
England, the English King ordered ten knight bannerets and
forty young bachelor knights to be prepared and equipped,
and he sent them, at great expense, on this side of the sea,
directly to Valenciennes, and he sent the Bishop of Lincoln,
who was a very valiant man, with them, in order to treat
with those lords of the Empire whom the Count of Hainnault
had named to them, and in order to do all that he and

8. Froissart, *Chroniques*, 2, 371–72.

John, his brother, should counsel. When they had come to Valenciennes, everyone regarded them with great wonder, for the beautiful and great estate which they maintained, without any sparing, no more than if the body of the king was there in his own proper person, by which they acquired great favor and great renown. And there were among them many bachelors, each one of whom had one eye covered by a cloth through which nothing could be seen. And it was said that they had vowed to some ladies in their country that they would never see with more than one eye until they should have done some deeds of prowess within the realm of France, nor were they willing to make any answer at all to those who asked them about it; thus everyone was very astonished. When they were sufficiently feasted and honored at Valenciennes, by the Count of Hainnault, by Sir John, his brother, by the gentlemen and knights of the country, and also by the burghers and ladies of Valenciennes, the said Bishop of Lincoln and the greater part of them turned toward the Duchy of Brabant, by the counsel of the above-mentioned Count. The Duke feasted them sufficiently, as he well knew how to do.

There are, of course, differences between these passages. Jordan is among the most sententious of aristocratic chroniclers although "high sentence" is common in all except Froissart. The passage from Jordan's chronicle is largely dramatic. It presents a direct confrontation of characters. But again this is not unusual. The passage from Froissart, on the other hand, is more detailed than most aristocratic chronicles, and less inclined to drama. These differences are manifestations of individuality within a common tradition and are not essential. The common tradition from which the two chronicles arose is apparent in spite of them.

Two characteristics are chiefly responsible for the similarity of aristocratic chronicles. First, they are narratives. Even the passage from Jordan communicates a push of subsequent actions forcing these present actions offstage. In this characteristic, aristocratic chronicles differ sharply from clerical ones, which were not, properly speaking, narrative at all. They were written as collections of incidents or events, and the clerical chronicler simply did not see a basic continuity of action. The aristocratic chroniclers, on the other hand, were primarily concerned with relating this continuous action, "this interminable tapeworm," as E. M. Forster has aptly called it, of things happening in time.[9]

The second characteristic must be considered in conjunction with the first. The actions with which the aristocratic chroniclers were concerned, being ordered more or less chronologically, were habitually reported in the most elementary relationship to each other. They were either juxtaposed without an explicit relationship or they were conjoined in the simple relationship indicated by the connectives "and" and "then." "This happened, and this happened, and then this happened"—such is the basic narrative pattern.

There are, of course, obvious kinds of modifications; otherwise these chronicles would be unreadable. Statements might be elaborated or amplified by other statements in a parallel relationship:[10]

> About this same time, it happened that Sir Broquart de Fenestrages, who had been of aid to the Duke of Normandy and the French against the English and Navarrese, *and had helped to cast down and discomfort them, and to drive them out of their fortresses in Champagne,* had been very badly paid for his commitments, and there was owing to him and his people a good thirty thousand francs.

The italicized lines are simply an amplification of what has gone before, enriching the narrative without moving it forward. The preceding "who" clause has the same sort of function.

Old French had connectives other than "and" and "then," of course (even though they are frequently very difficult to distinguish in their significations). The continuation of the passage quoted above illustrates the limited use which was ordinarily made of these other connections:[11]

> And feeling angry himself, he sent certain men instead of himself to Paris before the Duke of Normandy, to remind

---

9. E. M. Forster, *Aspects of the Novel* (New York, Harcourt, Brace and Co., 1927), p. 50.

10. Froissart, *Chroniques, 6,* 191–92. Italics added.

11. Ibid., p. 192.

> him of the matter of Sir Broquart and his companions; and
> he did not answer them particularly to their liking, *but*
> paid them with bad language, and they returned to the knight
> without accomplishing anything. *When* Sir Broquart . . .

The "but" (*mais*) and the "when" (*quant*) do not mark any sharp
departure from the simple, additive relationships generally characteristic of the passage. The first merely sets up an antithesis
which functions as amplification; the second simply functions to
preserve narrative sequence. Neither of these narrative variants
modifies the additive character of the aristocratic chronicle significantly.

Taken together, these two characteristics suggest that the aristocratic chronicle owes its organization not primarily to a perceptual mode but to a value system. Again, comparison can be
useful. The traditional modern narrative, which English-speaking
countries owe to Shakespeare (assisted by Marlowe), has as its
reason for being the conviction that meaning lies within the
relationship of events. These narratives answer the question, "how
did such-and-such come to be?" (or, "why is it true that . . . ?")
by an examination of the very causal processes by which it actually
came about. The origin of Shakespeare's history plays, for instance,
is very clearly, as E. M. W. Tillyard has shown, an Elizabethan
truism: "usurpation has its consequences."[12] But the plays do not
state that truism; they examine it and attempt to understand it
by scrutinizing its workings. The preexistent perceptual mode
views the human world as causal process.

But this is not the case in the aristocratic chronicles; the
"and–then" gives these chronicles their unmistakable character.
Both "and" and "then" are simple connectives, and neither has
causal force. A narrative which achieves its character merely by
connecting actions by "and" cannot explain anything, because
the relationships it establishes are limited and purely temporal.
One can hence accept as established what a critical reader surely
suspects upon first reading, that these interminable action sequences were valued for themselves.

The nonexplanatory character of these chronicles is also con-

12. E. M. W. Tillyard, *Shakespeare's History Plays* (New York, Mac-
millan, 1946).

firmed by the statements of the chroniclers themselves (for what
such statements are worth).[13] Froissart declares:[14]

> In order that the honorable enterprises and noble adventures
> and feats of arms which have come to pass in the wars of
> France and England, may be related in a notable way and
> held in perpetual remembrance, by which the nobles (*preux*)
> should have example to encourage them to do well, I wish
> to deal with and record a history and matter for great praise.

The other aristocratic chronicles are self-proclaimed accounts of
great men. In his prologue to the *Roman de Rou,* Master Wace
says, "In honour of the second Henry, of the line of Roul, I have
told the tale of Roul, of his noble parentage, of Normandy that
he conquered, and the prowess that he showed."[15] The herald of
Chandos says,[16]

> Now may God let me come to it [the subject],
> Because I wish to make it my study
> To compose and record the life
> Of the most valiant prince of the world,
> And when one searches the globe,
> There never was such a one since the time of Claris,
> Julius Caesar and Arthur,
> As you can hear,
> But you must listen to it with a good heart.

It is, in fact, a mark of the aristocratic chronicle that it aims to
celebrate, not to explain, the action with which it is concerned.
An explanation that may occur along the way is never the point
of the narrative.

---

13. It seems to me some sort of negative value can be attached to such
statements; a chronicle, or a romance, is not apt to attempt more than it
claims. On the other hand, it may very well claim an objective to which
the text is not, in fact, aimed. Jordan of Fantosme, for instance, says in
his preface (*Chronique,* l. 4, p. 202), "I hold him as wise who corrects himself by others." But this is merely a part of Jordan's indiscriminate love of
sententiousness and has nothing to do with the chronicle he has written.

14. Froissart, *Chroniques, 2, 4.*

15. *Roman de Rou,* p. 5.

16. Mildred K. Pope and Eleanor C. Lodge, eds. and trans., *Life of
the Black Prince by the Herald of Sir John Chandos* (Oxford, The
Clarendon Press, 1910), ll. 46–54, p. 2.

Perhaps even more significant to the nature of these chronicles as vehicles of value is a peculiar doubling pattern found inter-mittently in all of them. Here is a typical example from the *Life of the Black Prince* concerning the action immediately prior to the battle of Poitiers:[17]

> In such wise did the Prince sojourn
> In Gascony, and he made stay there
> The space of eight months or more.
> Very great were his virtues.
> When it came toward summer
> Then he assembled his power;
> Afterwards he made a ride again
> Into Saintonge, I assure you,
> Into Perigord and into Quercy,
> And he came as far as Romorantin.
> He took there the tower by assault,
> Also the Lord Boucicaut,
> And the great Lord of Craon,
> And of others a very great abundance.
>
> . . .
>
> Afterward he rode into Berry
> And through Gascony also,
> And up to Tours in Tourayne.

To this point, of course, this is typical, "and–and" running narra-tive. But the next section is something else again:[18]

> Then, and it is a thing most certain,
> The news to King John came,
> About which he made a great complaint,
> And he said that he would prize himself little
> Should he not take great vengeance.
> Then he ordered to assemble the power
> Of the whole realm of France.
> Nor did there remain there duke nor count
> Nor baron who was of any account,
> Whom he did not have brought together,

17. Ibid., ll. 703–23, p. 21.
18. Ibid., ll. 724–66, pp. 21–22.

> And, as I have heard tell,
> The assembly was made at Chartres.
> A noble host was brought together
> Because, as the list tells,
> He had there more than ten thousand men.
> From Chartres they have departed
> And they rode, right so,
> All together toward Tours.
> The Prince heard the news,
> Which seemed to him good and fair.
> He took his way toward Poitiers
>
>   . . .
>
> And then King John rode
> So well that he came before the Prince
> And the one host beheld the other,
> And, as I have understood,
> The one lodged before the other,
> And they camped so very near each other
> That they watered, by Saint Peter,
> Their horses at one river.

This kind of alternating reportage, first of one side and then of the other, is a marked characteristic of the whole genre of aristocratic chronicles.[19] Such passages are invariably found in prelude to a confrontation, usually military, and their function is obviously dramatic; they serve to heighten the significance of the action with which they are concerned. They confer value.

In short, the aim of the aristocratic chronicle is to celebrate the values implicit in the actions they relate. But this observation raises a problem. Explanations of action such as are found in the clerical chronicles necessarily imply a mode of perception, since to explain, in this sense, requires an a priori expectation of how things are related. This has already been argued in the introduction and

19. For similar alternating narratives see the *Chronique* of Jordan, ll. 60 ff., pp. 208 ff., and *The Chronicle of Pierre de Langtoft, RS,* 47:2, 313–15. Froissart is full of such alternating narratives (see his accounts of the battles of Crécy and Poitiers, as well as of the abortive battle of Vironfosse, for example). This is the more curious in that Froissart is much more interested in the pageantry of chivalry than in its heroic stance-taking, of which the alternating narrative is a reflection.

demonstrated in the second chapter. But does an account oriented toward values have the same status? Is the aristocratic chronicler describing action as he sees it, or is he consciously ordering it as he wishes it to be?

I should perhaps say immediately that the way of ordering experience described in the earlier part of this chapter reflects a mode of perception as surely as do the comparable clerical materials. But this conclusion may not be established to the reader's satisfaction until the end of the next chapter. There are, however, kinds of evidence bearing on the problem, even though not conclusively, which need to be considered at this point. A good place to begin is with the relationship between aristocratic and clerical chronicles.

Mixed Modes of Perception

In any overall view of medieval chronicles, the most striking and surely the most significant fact is the degree to which these parallel ways of seeing the world maintained their independence from each other. However, some cross-influence is to be found, and it bears directly on the problem of the perceptual nature of aristocratic chronicle writing.

By and large, this influence went in one direction; aristocratic modes of perception influenced clerical chronicles. This is not as paradoxical as it might appear. The clerical world was a closed one; clerical modes of perception were absorbed through extensive contact with Latin literature. I know of no chronicle reflecting, even faintly, clerical organization that does not at the same time reflect training in Latin. Furthermore, the intellectual world of the aristocrat seems to have been more resistant to alien notions than the clerical. Aristocratic writings touching on clerical subjects such as religion always essentially falsified them (aristocratic accounts of crusading are an example[20]), but clerical writers were receptive to aristocratic values.[21] Hence the rare examples of cleri-

20. Ambroise's *The History of the Holy War*, in Stone, *Three Old French Chronicles*, is a good example. Except for religious formalities to be endured with grace and such oddments of magical powers (from the aristocrat's point of view) as the discovery of the Holy Lance, the religious significance of the enterprise escaped the author entirely. Aristocratic literature as a whole suggests that he was typical in this respect.

21. See Chapter 5, pp. 163–64.

cal influence upon aristocratic chronicles, discussed below, are not integrated into other parts of the text but appear to be simply interpolated into it.[22]

The reverse is not true. Most educated clerks, surely, were aristocratic in their modes of perception before they learned any Latin, and new ways of seeing the world did not completely invalidate old ones, even in the perception of human action.

The presence of aristocratic modes of perception in generally clerical chronicles can only be seen in lengthy quotations, and hence one example, drawn from the *Gesta Stephani*, must suffice. Here is the *Gesta's* account of the uprisings which followed the arrival of Queen Matilda in England:[23]

> At that time (*ea tempestate*) there was a certain baron Fitz Count . . . who was extremely delighted at their arrival and, after strengthening an impregnable castle that he had at Wallingford, rebelled against the king with spirit and great resolution, assisted by a very large body of soldiers. Miles likewise . . . broke the faith he had pledged to the king and rose against him.

To this point the structure is clearly clerical; the arrival of Matilda is an action (against the ground of a more or less settled England) to which the quoted passage is the consequence. There follows a passage (here omitted) which is also clerical—a nonchronological and generalized account of the depredations of the said Miles, an account which simply extends the consequence further. But what follows that is not of the same order:[24]

> But King Stephen was quite unconquered and unbroken by all the sea of troubles that pressed on him, and gathering his forces into a large army, he boldly tried to overcome his enemies one by one. And first, indeed, coming to Wallingford with an innumerable host, he proposed to close them in with a tenacious and unbreakable siege, when forestalled by the more useful counsel of his barons, he gave up for the time

22. See the discussion of the *Vita Edwardi Secundi*, pp. 94–97.
23. *Gesta Stephani*, p. 60.
24. Ibid., pp. 61–62.

what he had conceived in his mind. [Barons argue against siege] . . . Therefore, they said, it was a convenient plan . . . that with two castles constructed and garrisoned by a sufficient number of men to maintain the siege, he himself might turn away to overcoming others elsewhere. . . .

So hastily putting up two castles, he made his way with his whole force towards a castle called Trowbridge . . . But (*verum*) on his appointed way a wonderful stroke of good fortune befell him, in that he both took by storm the castle of Cerney . . . and received the surrender of the castle at the town of Malmesbury . . . But (*verum*) seeing that the chances of war are changeful, and Fortune, as she makes our world revolve, now raises a man to the heights and soon dashes him down to the depths, after a success of such joyous presage a sudden and unexpected disaster followed for the king.

This is not, of course, the prose one finds in aristocratic chronicles, but at the same time the overall "and–and" narrative structure is sufficiently apparent, particularly in view of the vague connective force that *verum* carried in medieval Latin. The business about Fortune (which was shortly thereafter turned into Providence by the author) is, I would suggest, the writer straining after his ordinary perceptual mode, toward a ground–action–consequence organization of the clerical mode of perception, but the passage is nevertheless basically a running narrative.

Such passages are not common in clerical chronicles, and they are, furthermore, not always easy to distinguish from complex forms of the prevalent triadal structure of the clerical mode of perception. The difficulty arises because the Latin to which these writers were accustomed, with its ablatives and multitude of subordinating connectives, was excellently suited to the clerical mode of perception but poorly suited to the aristocratic. Hence stylistic necessities might easily obscure an aristocratic mode of perception. The best test is this: an aristocratic narrative establishes a real temporal connection between its elements; as a consequence, there is a kind of swing to such narratives, a forward movement. The clerical mode of perception, on the other hand, is fundamentally antitemporal; it is always endeavoring to force its materials into static, self-limiting relationships.

It is possible, of course, that the shadowy reflections of the aristocracy in clerical chronicles are in reality incompletely digested written or oral communications from aristocratic sources. It seems more probable that ordinarily the specter was out of the chronicler's own past and represents his original perception of the world. In these chronicles the aristocratic mode of perception is almost invariably found in narrations of conflict, exactly where life was most charged with values for the aristocrat.[25] The most common relic of the aristocratic view is the alternating narrative, by which opposing forces are traced alternately, step by step, toward a confrontation. Since such a confrontation involved the deepest aristocratic values, it is likely that the past of the chronicler, rather than his sources, accounts for the appearance of aristocratic modes at just such points.

But the above passage does more than show the penetration of a clerical document by an aristocratic narrative. It at least suggests that the aristocratic narrative was a mode of perception and not merely the reflection of a system of values. King Stephen was, for the author, an heroic man breasting a sea of troubles. But in the passage, and in the *Gesta* as a whole, there is no impulse to celebrate Stephen's heroism. The author was a cleric who, unlike many of his fellow ecclesiastics, sincerely lamented the occasion for heroism. Hence we see in the *Gesta* the aristocratic mode of perception, in Latin guise, already divorced from the value system it ordinarily reflected.

However, the *Vita Edwardi Secundi* provides better evidence that the aristocratic style was truly a mode of perception and not merely an assertion of values. The author was apparently a lawyer with a foot in both worlds,[26] and his narrative puts the running aristocratic style to very peculiar uses indeed.

It will be useful to begin where little complexity is found and, hence, the basic pattern is most apparent. Here is part of the account of Edward's behavior following Bannockburn:[27]

25. See Chapter 4, pp. 111–13.
26. *Vita Edwardi Secundi,* ed. N. Denholm-Young, *NMC,* pp. xix–xxviii. It is perhaps worth noting that, amid many quotations from Scripture and Civil Law, particularly, there are only two definite quotations from classical authors, one from Horace and one from Martial, with a possible echo of Lucan also.
27. Ibid., p. 57.

After this the King, with the advice of his men, Berwick having been garrisoned, went to York, and there he took counsel
with the Earl of Lancaster and the other magnates, and sought
a remedy for his misfortunes. The earls said that the Ordinances had not been observed, and for that reason events had
turned out badly for the King, both because the King had
sworn to stand to the Ordinances, and because the archbishop
had excommunicated all who opposed them. They affirmed
that for this reason nothing could be done well unless the
Ordinances were observed more fully. The King said that he
was prepared to do everything ordained for the common
good, and he promised that he would observe the Ordinances
in good faith. The earls said that nothing seemed to be done
while something remained to do, but if the Ordinances ought
to be observed, it was necessary to ask for their execution. The
King conceded their execution; he denied nothing to the earls.

This is typical running narrative, even to the amplifying clause
concluding the section, and it moves as fast as any aristocratic
chronicle. The lengthy account of the battle of Bannockburn
and its aftermath[28] is related in a style which swings along almost
as briskly as the passage just quoted.

On the whole, however, the *Vita* does not move so rapidly.
Much of the book, especially toward the end, achieves a kind of
density by elaboration. In the report of the embassy of 1317 to the
papacy, for instance,[29] the king's requests are laid out in parallel
sentences as though they constituted a narrative, although they are
in fact a kind of amplification. The pope's response is handled
similarly. Such passages have narrative structure without narrative
intent. But another kind of organization which is even more common can be illustrated by the passage that opens the chronicle:[30]

Edward the First after the Conquest, paying his debt to nature
on the day of the Translation of St. Thomas in the thirty-fifth
year of his reign, his son Edward II, young and strong in body,
and being about twenty-three years of age, took over the
kingdom. He did not at all fulfill the ambition of his father,

28. Ibid., pp. 50–56.
29. Ibid., pp. 78–79.
30. Ibid., p. 1.

but directed his plans to other ends. He called back Piers
Gaveston, who had recently abjured England at the command
of his father. This Piers had been the most intimate and
highly favored member, as soon became abundantly clear, of
the young Edward's household when the latter was Prince of
Wales and the old king was still alive.

These four sentences, in spite of their Latinate subordination, set
up a running narrative; but even upon first reading one may
detect something peculiar. The first two sentences manifest a
straightforward, essentially narrative connection. The third sentence appears to be merely an amplification of the second clause of
the preceding sentence. The fourth sentence, beginning, "This
Piers," moves still further from the narrative line implicit in the
first two sentences. This is running narrative, but it runs eccentrically—into the subject, rather than along with it. What follows
is also peculiar:[31]

For the young Lord King gave to the Lord Piers, returned
from exile, the earldom of Cornwall, with the approval of
some of the magnates, namely Henry de Lacy, Earl of Lincoln,
and others. And indeed this same Earl Henry de Lacy, when it
was doubted whether the king could legally alienate the
aforesaid earldom, when he held with the crown, said that
the king could, for other kings had done this twice before.
Nevertheless, the greater part of the barons of the land did
not agree, both because Piers was an alien born in Gascony
and because of envy. For the magnates of the land hated him,
because he alone had grace in the eyes of the king and ruled
as if he were a second king, to whom all were subject and
none equal. Also, almost all the land, great and small and old,
hated him and foretold ill of him.

In this passage the first statement is set up as evidence of Edward's
favoritism, mentioned earlier, but the second part, about Henry de
Lacy, pulls off from the narrative direction. This second part is
then substantiated by an elaboration, and we swing to the opposite
point of view—that of the barons who hated Piers—which does

31. Ibid.

not connect at all with what has gone before. The last sentence extends the previous one.

This peculiar movement is due to the fact that the writer is interested in analysis, but the aristocratic mode of perception is utterly foreign to analysis. Hence sentence after sentence is written as though it bore an "and–then" relationship to what has gone before, when in fact it does not bear that relationship at all. An aristocratic chronicler could not have written this passage because he would not have been interested in such analysis. A clerical chronicler would have organized it in a radically different fashion. The *Vita* has a foot in each world.

The *Vita* shows conclusively that the aristocratic style was not merely a reflection of aristocratic values. The purpose of the *Vita* is not to celebrate anything; it is to give a sober account of the lamentable misbehavior of Edward toward his earls. The author used the running narrative style because he saw this shape in his materials: the aristocratic style was his way of seeing. It is very likely, then, that this style was also a perceptual mode for the strictly aristocratic, Anglo-Norman chroniclers. Thus we must assume that the aristocratic class as a whole saw life ordered by such perceptual framework.

Explanation in the Aristocratic Chronicle

The previous chapter has shown that, at least from the middle of the twelfth century, the clerical chronicle was intermittently explanatory. Furthermore, its interest in explanation was analogous to the modern, in that its ground–action–consequence structure was genuinely aimed at the "how" of a human (or a scientific) event, even though its unfamiliar form has frequently misled modern scholars. It can be argued, I think, that this kind of explanation was implicitly the major objective of the fully developed clerical chronicle—an objective largely frustrated by the resistance of the materials.

But the situation is otherwise with the aristocratic chronicle. Explanation was here not the object; indeed, explanation as defined above, as an attempt to get at the "how" of an event, was totally alien to such chronicles. This does not mean that they are simply interminable narratives. It means that these chronicles account for sequences of action—explain them, because there is no more suitable term—in very different ways from those of the clerical chronicler.

First, the aristocratic chronicler located an action in a human will. In this passage from Jordan, the action is the rebellion of Prince Henry, in alliance with France, against Henry II:[32]

> Now rides the Count Philip with his great host,
> And wastes Normandy by wood and by plain.
> You would never hear King Henry complain of it one time,
> Nor seek any occasion to delay the war.
> Much has the young king [Prince Henry] striven against
>   him, who is well-pleased
> That he has still at his command the barons of Brittany.
>   When his father heard this he was downcast and angry,
> And swears his oath that wrongly it was ever conceived,
> And says to his knights: "Lords, now hear me:
> Never in my life was I so sorry . . ."

Over and over one finds this kind of movement in aristocratic chronicles: a line of action is interrupted, almost gratuitously, by speeches and councils which appear to a modern reader to have no function. But for the medieval aristocrat a line of action was not complete until it had been located in a particular human will. In the passage quoted above we have a line of action undertaken by the French (prefaced also by speeches). The counteraction of the English was not accepted as a matter of course; its origin must be shown in the will of Henry II. The interminable councils with their heroic speeches, characteristic of all aristocratic chronicles, were hence, among other things, explanatory.[33] They locate the origin of the ensuing line of action for the reader.

Thus when Froissart undertook his long account of the civil war in Flanders, he explained that it originated in the pride and hatred that several of the chief towns bore to each other, which in turn originated in envy. When he came to describe the actual progress of the conflict, he narrowed his focus; lines of action

32. Jordan of Fantosme, *Chronique*, ll. 120–29, pp. 212–14.
33. The response to action was also a moment of great personal value; see Chapter 4, pp. 117–19.

were seen as originating in the wills of the successive leaders of
the rebellious townsmen and, more vaguely, in the will of the
Count of Flanders.[34] Similarly, Pierre de Langtoft set up a challenge–response passage concerning a Welsh uprising:[35]

> The year is given in the rubric above,
> When David of Wales went about playing the fox;
> With Llewellyn his brother he is accorded, in order to
> Disinherit the king and his stinking [punez] child;
> These have smashed his peace and broken covenant;
> They overrun his people, they burn in passing,
> They throw down his castles which they find standing.
> The king makes his barony to be sent for immediately,
> The barons come to him from Northumberland,
> The Southerners are there, no one holds back,
> They prepare their expedition against the two tyrants.

The aristocratic chronicler did not see a conflict as having a structure of its own. Each party to a conflict pursued his line of action,
which he initiated by an act of will. The opposing forces in a
conflict hence remain distinct from one another because their
actions were seen as manifestations of individual wills and not
as a part of an enveloping structure.

The kind of action that interested the aristocrat happened because someone willed it, and at times it was worthwhile to report
a motive for that willing. But neither the occasional explanation
of motive nor the habitual attribution of sequences of action to
particular human wills reflected any great curiosity about the
principles at work in the world, even the human world in which
the chronicler was interested. And neither seriously modified the
markedly narrative structure of these chronicles. The narrative
existed for its own sake.

In some odd way, the narrative itself was a kind of substitute
for explanation, as in a couple of instances in Froissart where one
narrative was answered by another in a kind of explanatory relationship. The first is found in the section devoted to the Count of
Foix. Froissart, visiting at the count's court, asked a squire about

34. Froissart, *Chroniques,* 9, 158 ff.
35. Pierre de Langtoft, *Chronicle,* p. 176. ("Punez" might mean
"younger" in this context also.)

the remarkable knowledge that the count displayed, instantly, concerning distant events. The squire "explained" this phenomenon not directly but by a detailed narrative about a familiar spirit that had become the servant of someone else entirely. He asserted no connection between the count and his story; the story simply stood in lieu of an explanation.[36]

The second instance is reported in connection with the attempt of some besieged North Africans to surprise the crusading French army of 1390 by means of a night raid. The North Africans were frustrated in the first place by the appearance of the Virgin—one of Froissart's rare allusions to the supernatural. But they were further frustrated by the barking of a dog:[37]

> Among other things, I was told that the Genoese cross-bowmen had brought from beyond the sea a dog in their company, and they did not know from whence he had come, and no one claimed this dog for himself. This dog had done and was doing good service for the whole host, because the Saracens could not come to them quietly, nor could they skirmish secretly, without the dog creating such a great uproar that he aroused those sleeping, and all the people knew well that when the dog yapped and bayed, that the Saracens were coming, so that one was able to meet them, and the Genoese called it the dog of Our Lady. Again at the hour that this *significance* came against the host, the dog was not idle, but created in a very disorderly fashion a great uproar and a great din.

The narrative impulse behind this explanation is manifest; we would have gotten a biography of the dog, if Froissart had known it. Both instances offer, in effect, brief chronicles in lieu of explanations; to explain something, for Froissart, was to relate the sequence of actions leading up to the thing to be explained or a sequence of comparable actions. Presumably Froissart's audience had a similar point of view.

But how foreign explanation was to the aristocratic chronicle (except in the limited sense described above) is best shown by recourse to the *Vita Edwardi Secundi.* The *Vita* is thoroughly, if

36. Froissart, *Chroniques, 11,* 189–201.
37. Ibid., *15,* 234–35.

peculiarly, aristocratic in its mode of perception, but at the same time it is as moralistic and concerned to judge action as any chronicle I know. Particularly in the later pages of the book, the narrative is continually interrupted by long passages commenting upon the action. But the significant fact is that such passages always stand outside the narrative. Here, for instance, is a characteristic approach to the understanding of history, concerning the ecclesiastical aid of 1316:[38]

> It indeed ought to be feared lest a contribution of this sort, which burdens the church, should lead the Lord King into ruin. For the goods of the church are the goods of paupers. Never has the spoliation of the poor, never has the spoliation of the church, had a favorable auspices. Certainly under Pharaoh, although by the royal ordinance all were urged generally to pay a fifth part, nevertheless priests were exempt from the observance of this burdensome decree. Also, in the book of Numbers, as a figure of perpetual liberty Pharaoh ordered that the priestly tribe should be free from every public office, though subject to the judgment of the supreme pontiff.

Secular history might be used the same way. Concerning the estrangement between the Earl of Lancaster and the king, and the king's deliberations upon it, he reports:[39]

> Some said: "It is right that he who scorns to obey his lord's commands shall purge his contumacy, and as a perjurer lose his fief if he holds one. Let the king therefore pursue and take his despiser, and when he is taken put him in prison or exile him." But others said: "It is no small matter to take the Earl of Lancaster. The Scots will support him, and a great part of Wales; it is better to proceed another way, and treat beforehand of a form of agreement. For it is very clear from the history of the Britons, how full of perils is civil discord. For that Julius Caesar subdued the kingdom of

38. *Vita Edwardi Secundi,* p. 77.
39. Ibid., pp. 80–81. A similar sort of explanation is to be found in the *Chronicle* of Pierre de Langtoft, by which the largesse of King Arthur is used to explain the notable lack of success of Edward II. *RS, 47:2, 296–98.*

Britain, that the Saxon race drove out the Britons and seized the kingdom, that the Normans in their turn assumed the governance of England, all these things are known to have resulted from a like discord."

History, for the author of the *Vita,* provided not examples but analogies of a most elementary sort. The link between the historical incident and the one being commented upon was some sort of aphorism at loose in the world and prior to both of them. Hence meaning was not implicit in an action sequence, it was implicit in the relationship between one sort of incident and another. As a consequence, explanation always constituted an interruption, and very nearly an irrelevance, to the narrative itself.

The difference between the medieval and the modern is handsomely illustrated by another passage of the *Vita.* The baronial opposition to Piers Gaveston and his influence upon Edward II was led, in its later stages, by the Earl of Lancaster, and because he was the most powerful of the baronial party, he took it upon himself to behead Piers when the opportunity offered. After some years of continual friction, the earl unhappily fell into the hands of the king, with consequences which were entirely foreseeable. The author of the *Vita* remarks,[40]

> Perhaps a hidden cause, not immediate but remote (*preterita*), punished the earl. The Earl of Lancaster at one time bore off the head of Peter of Gaveston, and now by the command of the king, the Earl of Lancaster has lost his head.

Surely this is one of the few explanations to be found in medieval chronicles with which a modern historian might entirely agree. And he might use the *Vita* to reconstruct the process by which the one axing led to the other. But this process was entirely invisible to the author of the *Vita* himself. He continues:

> Thus, perhaps not unjustly, the Earl received measure for measure, as it is written in Holy Scripture: "For with the same measure that ye mete withal it shall be measured to you again." Thus Abner killed Asahel, striking him under

40. *RS,* 47:2, 126–27.

the fifth rib, but Abner did not escape, for he afterwards perished by a similar wound.

The author of the *Vita* did not see these two notorious events as directly connected; they were connected by an aphorism which underlies all historical examples.

But the chief value of the *Vita* in this connection is that it illustrates the limitations of the aristocratic chronicle. Its author had no way of integrating the clerical and the aristocratic perceptual worlds. The aristocratic modes of perception by which he saw the significant action around him did not permit clerical kinds of explanation; such explanation could only be introduced at the expense of the narrative, since it was irrelevant to it.

This is not to say that the medieval aristocrat was mindless and did not reason after his own fashion, for reason he did, and at times very well. The aristocratic mind often succeeded in establishing complicated networks of relationships bearing upon a single action or objective. Illustrative passages are particularly common in Froissart because his narrative is the most leisurely. The Duke of Lancaster's account of his reasons for desiring a peace with France, referred to previously, is typical of aristocratic reasoning:[41]

> I, John Froissart, the author of this history, do not know the story well enough to relate it properly, nor, further, to determine whether he was wrong or right, but it was told to me thus, that because the Duke of Lancaster saw his two daughters married above him and outside the realm of England, the one the Queen of Spain and the other Queen of Portugal, he was greatly inclined to peace, especially because he felt that his son-in-law who had his daughter, the young King of Spain, was yet insecure with his men, and, if he wished to enjoy and possess his heritage and the profits of Spain peacefully, it was fitting that he should hold the peace and alliance which they had with the realm of France, which those of England could not disturb; and, if they should break it by any chance, soon the French would make the kingdom of Spain suffer for it, because they had their entrances to it all open, as well through the realm of Aragon, of which

41. Froissart, *Chroniques, 15,* 81.

Madame Yoland of Bar was Queen and a good Frenchwoman, who governed at that time all the kingdom of Aragon and Catalonia, as well as through the countries of Bearn and the Basques, because the Viscount of Chateaubon, who was the heir of the Count Gaston of Foix, had also sealed and sworn to the King of France. Thus the French had many good entrances through which to enter Spain without fear of the King of Navarre, who, besides, did not wish to anger the King of France his cousin german, and besides Sir Peter of Navarre, his brother, remained near the King, and he would effectively break up whatever disputes should arise between the King of France and the King of Navarre, because he was a good Frenchman and loyal; nor could the princes be at all contrary in this. And all these conceptions Duke John of Lancaster thought about, and he showed them at the time to his young son, the Count of Derby.

This is very careful calculation. It is very unmodern both because there is no sense of flux and movement in the relationships being analyzed and because the human wills operative at every step in the sequence of events seem to be conceived in an elementary way. But the passage still reflects a demanding kind of mental activity. This kind of mental activity, it should be noted, is embodied pre-eminently in the game of chess; it is no accident that chess was so very popular among the aristocracy in the later Middle Ages.

Although an undergraduate can read aristocratic chronicles and romances and take some pleasure in them, close scrutiny shows that they are even more remote from our own way of seeing than the clerical mode of perception. In his own fashion, the clerk could ask the sort of "why" questions characteristic of the modern approach, and he would attempt to answer them. The body of clerical speculation on natural phenomena, however erroneous it may have been (and in view of the current scholarly deference to things medieval, it is salutary to remind ourselves from time to time that it was almost entirely erroneous), bears a relationship to modern speculation and thus relates contemporary investigators to the medieval clerk. There is no corresponding body of materials relating us to the medieval aristocrat.

It would be an understatement, an inaccuracy, to say that the medieval aristocrat was not interested in understanding human action. The possibility of such an understanding (in the clerical or the modern sense) simply did not exist for him; it was precluded by the way in which he saw the world.

Alfred North Whitehead has argued that two antithetical notions lie behind all experience—the sense of fact, of the material of our perceptions being really existent, and the sense of importance, by which we discriminate among facts.[42] We can go further and say that our sense of importance is in large measure taught to us as a mode of perception, and that this mode of perception profoundly affects the very stuff of reality given by the sense of fact. The aristocratic and clerical modes of perception were not simply different ways of ordering and evaluating the same human reality in which the clerk related objects in one way, the aristocrat in another. The aristocratic mode of perception permitted a kind of narrative organization of certain facts which the clerk could not effectively organize at all, while the clerical mode of perception could recognize causal relationships invisible to the aristocrat. Our sense of importance gives our human world the only shape it can have for us.

42. Alfred N. Whitehead, *Modes of Thought* (New York, Capricorn Books, 1958), pp. 5–27.

CHAPTER 4

The Aristocratic View of Human Nature

As the previous chapter has shown, a medieval aristocrat was not engaged in an attempt to understand the physical world around him, and his interest in the motives of his fellow aristocrats was limited to a very simple kind of anticipation of response. His attention was monopolized by that other serious human concern, values. Practically everything written beyond his ledger books was concerned, as were his chronicles, with proper human behavior. The medieval aristocrat was a kind of moralist, although his moralism was not always recognized by the ecclesiastics of the time.

This moralism, combined with a total lack of interest in speculation, meant that the aristocratic view—an implicit view, of course —could not consider man in terms of his innate powers or potentialities. Man was, instead, always considered teleologically, in light of those values and goals he regarded as a kind of immutable definition of proper human behavior;[1] they constituted the only meaningful definition of man. Because of this orientation, an understanding of the aristocratic conception of man must begin with an examination of the values that were the measure of man.

The aristocratic value system for the period from about 1100 to 1400 was that elaboration of feudalism known today as chivalry.

---

1. In the romances (*Havelok the Dane,* for instance), one occasionally finds a situation in which a hero's true nobility shines through humble circumstances. But there is never any sense of the writer being concerned with a generic question. The nobility of the hero is simply there, and the writer exploits the variety of situations his humble position makes possible.

This code was, of course, not entirely static during these three centuries. *L'Histoire de Guillaume le Marechal* is not precisely the same sort of book as the *Chroniques* of Froissart, nor was the *Chronique* of Jordan of Fantosme written from exactly the same point of view as the *Life of the Black Prince*. But the changes did not result from any essential innovation in the aristocratic value system. In England, at least, the decline of feudalism (and chivalry as well) was not occasioned by the appearance of a rival conception of the good; it came about because the old ideas lost their viability.[2] Chivalry was not overthrown; it turned into pageantry.

Human Good

The conception of good implicit in chivalry has been the subject of full discussion, if not full agreement.[3] The major difficulties can be resolved if one accepts the distinction that Sidney Painter has proposed with respect to French chivalry. He argues that we must recognize three distinct positions: feudal chivalry, religious chivalry, and courtly love.[4]

The system of values labeled "feudal chivalry" is overwhelmingly predominant in the aristocratic chronicles. There is no evidence that aristocrats in any numbers at all ever took seriously

2. The usual explanation for the decline of chivalry is the social and economic one; the changing shape of feudalism and the developing money economy, particularly, undermined chivalric relationships. See the excellent summary of this view by Arthur B. Fergusson, *The Indian Summer of English Chivalry* (Durham, University of North Carolina Press, 1960), pp. 3–32. But it seems to me the scholars who have particularly argued this point of view assume the priority of economic causes without due consideration of other possibilities. A part of the difficulty in evaluating the course of chivalry is the relative scarcity of narrative sources. Raymond Kilgour points out, for instance, that at the end of his career Froissart lamented the decline of chivalry under Richard II. Raymond L. Kilgour, *The Decline of Chivalry* (Cambridge, Cambridge University Press, 1937), p. 68. But similar lamentations would have been quite appropriate under Edward II or Henry III. Dozens of remarks by Matthew Paris, for instance, about Henry's lack of military ardor, would sound much like Froissart if expressed in the language of chivalry.

3. Hearnshaw briefly summarizes the traditional range of opinion in *Chivalry,* ed. Edgar Prestage (New York, Knopf, 1928), pp. 1–3.

4. Sidney Painter, *French Chivalry* (Ithaca, Cornell University Press, 1957).

the function of policeman for church and state[5] that clerical writers on religious chivalry envisaged for them. The chronicles concerned with the actual doings of men would seem to be sufficient evidence that a handbook explicating religious chivalry, such as Lull's *Le Libre del orde de cauayleria,*[6] was clerical propaganda, and ineffective propaganda at that. The reflections of courtly love in the later chronicles, particularly in Froissart, are only picturesque embroidery.

In short, the dominant conception of good in the aristocratic chronicles throughout the period under consideration was the ethical system Painter has called feudal chivalry. If one accepts the significance of chronicles in medieval intellectual history, it follows that feudal chivalry ordered men's lives on the most important level and provided the measure of failure and disorder.

Painter defines feudal chivalry by the qualities it demanded of the knight: prowess, loyalty, largesse, and courtesy.[7] The chivalrous knight, exercising his natural gifts, was vigorous in his assaults upon other knights, he was generous to others (of his own class[8]), and he behaved according to a fairly well-defined schedule of responses to particular situations. The capacity to assault other knights effectively was of course a gift of God to be cultivated assiduously in the tilting yard. But the other qualities were to be manifested in individual relationships. Loyalty dictated the knight's behavior toward his superiors; largesse was especially manifested toward inferiors. Courtesy was the quality most apparent in the knight's relationships with both his equals and his enemies, and during this period, of course, courtesy was also extended to define the knight's relationships with women—they did not fall precisely into either category.

Such a list is of course not exhaustive; Gervase Mathew, in a study of the chivalry of the late fourteenth century, adds

5. The phrase is Painter's—Ibid., p. 88.
6. Translated by William Caxton as *The Book of the Ordre of Chyvalry,* ed. Alfred P. Byles, *EETS,* Old Series, no. 168 (London, Oxford University Press, 1926).
7. Painter, *French Chivalry,* pp. 28–64.
8. It seems to me, although a marshaling of evidence would be tedious, that the aristocrat clearly distinguished between the gift-giving habitual in his own circle from almsgiving. The latter was done for his soul's sake, the former was honorific. His gifts to religious foundations perhaps partook of both motives.

"franchise" and "pitie";[9] innumerable passages assure us that the medieval aristocrat also cherished physical beauty as an ideal. Furthermore, at least by the late fourteenth century, these qualities, by reason of their honorific character, were rapidly losing their specific denotations.[10]

However, regardless of the exact list of attributes one proposes, it is clear that goodness for the medieval aristocrat was always to be found in specified status relationships. In the complicated maneuverings between William the Marshal and King John, for instance, *L'Histoire* presents William as a model of feudal loyalty.[11] But this loyalty was not between the man William and the man John; it was the loyalty of a vassal to a king. For both men feudal chivalry dictated a kind of behavior; they were not expected to behave with respect to each other but with respect to a situation whose proper behavior was prescribed. No cliché is more common in medieval history than the assertion that feudalism was a system built upon personal relationships, but unless "personal" is understood in a very special way, the cliché is not true: the personalism of the medieval aristocracy was actually very impersonal.

The same code that prescribed the form of relationships under certain circumstances required estrangement under others. The knight was obliged to be loyal to his feudal suzerain only so long as that suzerain behaved in a certain way toward him; otherwise the code of conduct might oblige him to go to war. It was surely in this light that Richard I regarded his war with Philip.[12] Courtesy, likewise, prescribed physical assault as well as forms of politeness, and the conditions under which largesse was appropriate did not presuppose any sort of human relationship.

9. Gervase Mathew, "Ideals of Knighthood in Late Fourteenth-Century England," *Studies in Medieval History Presented to Frederick Maurice Powicke* (Oxford, Oxford University Press, 1948), pp. 354–62.

10. See below, p. 125.

11. This was particularly apparent when loyalties had to be shared, as after the fall of Normandy (*L'Histoire de Guillaume le Marechal*, ll. 12935–13256, ed. Paul Meyer, *Société de l'histoire de France* [3 vols. Paris, Librairie Renouard, 1901], 2, 101–13); see the discussion by Sidney Painter in his valuable study, *William Marshal* (Baltimore, Johns Hopkins University Press, 1933), pp. 138–47. Secular chronicles are full of quarrels between king and barons which reflect the ambiguous demands of loyalty.

12. William of Newburgh, *Historia rerum anglicarum*, 5, xv; *RS*, 82:2, 455–56.

The feudal code could not be directed to the fostering of human relationships because it was directed toward another end: the personal honor of the aristocrat. But one must take care not to read a modern meaning into this medieval term, this *onor* as it is written in *L'Histoire*. In later times honor came to have, if not a negative meaning, at least a negative sort of function in human life. A gentleman of the eighteenth century, for instance, preserved his honor by not doing certain things and by not allowing certain things to be done to him. It was not honorable to lie, for instance, nor could the charge of lying be borne without loss of honor. Even in military matters in postmedieval times honor has generally implied a passive acceptance of responsibilities.

This conception of honor was of course not unknown in the Middle Ages; indeed, one's honor, viewed in this negative fashion, was even more demanding then than later. When a deputation of nobles attempting to control Henry III, for instance, asked for the support of the King's brother, Richard, he answered, "with an exceedingly fierce countenance and menacing words, swearing by the throat of God,"[13]

> "I will neither swear the oath which you require, nor will I make known to you the limit of my stay in England." And he added, "I have not an equal in England, for I am the son of the departed king and the brother of the present one, and I am Count of Cornwall. If, then, the nobles of England had wished to reform the deformed kingdom, they ought first to have sent for me, and not thus impetuously, without my connivance or presence, to have entered presumptuously on so difficult a business.

Richard's chief concern in this situation was his honor; for the barons to undertake any collective action without consulting him was an affront. Similarly, the eternal quarrels in the Middle Ages between kings and barons about the latter's right to give advice, so common in English history, were not merely quarrels about the distribution of power; the right to give counsel was honorific, and the barons of the king's council were obliged by their honor to defend that right. Kings might argue, on the other hand, that

13. Matthew Paris, *Chronica majora*, RS, 57:5, 733.

the royal dignity was diminished if they have no choice in the matter of counselors.

But honor was much more than this in the Middle Ages; honor was something a medieval aristocrat was expected to pursue positively and aggressively. "A long repose disgraces a young man," asserted the author of *L'Histoire* in connection with Prince Henry's request that he might go adventuring, and the Prince himself said to his father, the aging Henry II:[14]

> If it would not displease you,
> It would be very good for me and please me
> To go beyond the sea to amuse myself,
> For it could grieve and harm me much
> And it bores me very severely
> To remain here so long.
> I am not a hawk to be kept in a mew.
> A young man who is not active
> Can rise to no good:
> One ought to count him for nothing.

The heroic stature of William the Marshal was in great measure due to the fearsome amount of energy he expended in his younger years in the pursuit of honor,[15] and in the much-quoted scene in which he agreed to assume the regency for the young Henry III, it was the honor of the enterprise that moved him to undertake it.[16] A French writer, Philippe de Navarre, asserted, "he who passes his youth without exploit may have cause for great shame and grief."[17]

The orientation toward honor in medieval aristocratic thought has been generally recognized but usually underrated. Everything about medieval chronicles—clerical and aristocratic—tells us that honor was in one way or another the foremost value in the aristo-

14. *Guillaume le Marechal*, ll. 2409–18; *1*, 88–89.
15. See Painter, *William Marshal*, pp. 30–60.
16. *Guillaume le Marechal*, ll. 15655–98; *2*, 200–02. Painter, *William Marshal*, pp. 196–97, discusses the passage. Powicke argues that there were social and political motives in the Marshal's decision, but he admits that there is no evidence for this (*King Henry III and the Lord Edward* [2 vols. Oxford, Oxford University Press, 1947], *1*, 5).
17. Philippe de Navarre, *Les Quatre ages de l'homme,* ed. Marcel de Freville, Société des Anciens Textes Français (Paris, Firmin Didot, 1888), pp. 38–39. Quoted in Painter, *William Marshal*, p. 30.

cratic scheme. The best evidence of its importance was its function as a criterion: the good man was the one who was aggressive in the pursuit of honor. Thus Jordan of Fantosme says of Henry II:[18]

> [He was] the most honorable and conquering
> That was in any land since the time of Moses,
> Except only King Charles, whose power was great
> Through the twelve companions, Oliver and Roland.
> Thus there was not witnessed in fable nor in story
> Any king of his valor nor of his great power.

The death of King Richard, on the other hand, was an irreparable loss, because had he lived he would have conquered the whole world, Christian and pagan (the French excepted).[19] The writer of the *Vita Edwardi Secundi* remarked of his subject:[20]

> For our King Edward has now reigned six full years and has till now achieved nothing praiseworthy or memorable, except that by a royal marriage he has raised up for himself a handsome son and heir to the throne. How differently began King Richard's reign: before the end of the third year of his reign he had scattered far and wide the rays of his valour.

Comparable passages could be multiplied without profit; even clerical chroniclers habitually evaluated their kings in such terms.[21]

---

18. Jordan of Fantosme, *Chronique*, ll. 112–17; *RS*, 82:3, 212.

19. The terms of praise proposed by the writer of *L'Histoire* (ll. 11820–29; 2, 61) are of some interest:

> Richard, the courageous and the well-bred,
> The generous and the good giver,
> The enterprising and the conqueror,
> Who would have won all the prizes
> Of this world, if he had lived,
> And the greatness and the mastery,
> And the honor and the seignory
> Over the Saracens, over the Christians
> And over all the people of the world.

France is excepted from the universal empire in the following lines, undoubtedly because its king was Richard's sovereign.

20. *Vita Edwardi Secundi*, *NMC*, p. 39. I have used Denholm-Young's translation of the passage.

21. See Chapter 5, pp. 163–64.

The aristocracy of the twelfth century was unabashed in its commitment to heroic aggression as an essential element of the good life, but I know of nothing in later centuries exactly parallel to *L'Histoire's* lament upon Richard's untimely demise. Due, perhaps, to the influence of the Church, conflicts in the later centuries were presented as defensive; honor in its negative aspect was responsible for the continued political turbulence. The political equivalent of this reinterpretation of motives was the cliché that the king's function was to give protection against evildoers at home and enemies abroad—in other words, that his function was defensive.[22] But medieval peace treaties were ordinarily so ambiguous —often by design—that hostilities could be resumed by either party at any time with a sufficient color of virtue. To the end of the period, the nobility demanded that English kings provide frequent opportunities for military activity, and the kings cherished in their own times invariably did so.[23]

But the really interesting question remains: what, precisely, did the aristocrat pursue so diligently? Certainly honor meant, in part, reputation. The knight meant his deeds to be known, and seldom could he send his defeated adversaries back home as testimonials to his prowess, as did the hero of *The Prose Perceval*.[24] To be

22. See the address to his barons attributed to Edward I: "I am castle for you, and wall, and house (*Jo suy chastel pur ws, et mur, et mesoun*)." *The Chronicle of Pierre de Langtoft,* ed. Thomas Wright, *RS, 47:2,* 288–89. Skelton had recourse to the same argument in the *apologia* he wrote for Edward IV after the latter's death: "I was your king, and kept you from your foe." "On the Death of the Noble Prince, King Edward the Fourth," *The Complete Poems of John Skelton* (2nd ed. London, Dent, 1948), p. 2. Sir John Fortescue, decidedly under clerical influence, proposed that "to defende his reaume ayen þair enemies outwarde bi the swerde" was one of the two royal functions. Sir John Fortescue, *The Governaunce of England,* ed. Charles Plummer (London, Oxford University Press, 1926), p. 116. Further references are provided in the footnote to the Fortescue passage, pp. 201–02.

23. Giraldus reports that Philippe Augustus resolved to restore to France its boundaries at the time of Charlemagne; he was of course wildly applauded by his barons: "May he perish who imposes any impediment to such a prince, so noble-minded for restoring the rights of the kingdom." Giraldus Cambrensis, *De instructione principum,* Dist. III, ch. xxv; *Opera,* ed. George F. Warner, *RS, 21:8,* 294. Given this principle, a defensive war was possible at any time, virtually with anyone.

24. *The Romance of Perceval in Prose,* trans. Dell Skeels, University of Washington Publications in Language and Literature, 15 (Seattle, University of Washington Press, 1961), pp. 20, 35, 52.

talked of was at times an explicit motive of some of Froissart's
knights;[25] even more graphically, a messenger warned King
William of Scotland, "If you remain here much longer, / A bad
song will be sung of you."[26] But these are trivial indications of
the omnipresent aristocratic yearning for fame; the best evidence
is the very existence of the aristocratic chronicles. They were
written explicitly to apportion that fame.

But reputation was only a part of the aristocratic conception
of good. It is hard to formulate, but if a single word might suggest
this conception, that word would be "stance." The aristocrat found
his summum bonum in a kind of public posture taken with
regard to his own class; he was an actor inventing a script which
he hoped would turn out to be heroic. This is a difficult conception
for an educated man in the twentieth century; it is both too far
from us and too near—too far because the elaborate ceremony and
display of the medieval aristocrat seem ludicrous, too near because the equivalent concern for posture is all around us and seems
an innate human impulse. To understand the Middle Ages, we
must realize that a great many activities—the most important ones
—were pursued for their own sake, with no other end in view
beyond the public posture they permitted.

Medieval literature is filled with considerations of stance. In
the first place, it was the preeminent consideration in warfare,
where the knight's honor was most sharply tested. There are of
course some examples of absolute heroism pursued to its unfortunate end in aristocratic chronicles; one need only instance the
remarkable action of Gilis de Argenten at Bannockburn, who led
Edward II to safety and then returned to the hopeless battle and
death, declaring,[27]

> Sire, your [horse's] rein was committed to me; you are now
> in safety; there is your castle where your person may be safe.
> I am not accustomed to fly, nor do I want to do it in the
> future. I commend you to God.

25. "And thus [we] will be spoken of by all the world," Froissart,
Chroniques, *14*, 213.
26. Jordan of Fantosme, *Chronique*, l. 732; *RS*, *82:3*, 265.
27. *Scalacronica*, p. 143.

But Gilis' action was neither typical nor necessary. The action of Edward himself was much closer to the norm. He is said to have been led from the battle unwillingly. But since, according to the text, he still possessed a mace with which he beat off Scottish footsoldiers who would have detained him, there was clearly something pro forma about his reluctance to leave the scene.[28]

Over and over the modern reader observes honor functioning in a surprising way. At the Scottish King William's siege of Carlisle, for instance, a messenger arrived to announce the approach of an English army. William was counseled by his men,[29] "As he wished still to be honored, / He should leave the siege and go away at his own pleasure," which he did. In doing so, he apparently preserved his honor by preserving appearances. Having left before the other army arrived, he could seem to have wandered off absentmindedly, although both armies surely knew better.

A more striking example of the same conception is found in Froissart. The French trapped a German knight and his party in a kind of ambush. The German knight, Sir Reginald de Boullent, promptly struck down the leader of the French party and galloped off. However,[30]

> when he saw that they followed so closely that he was obliged to turn back or be blamed, he stopped in his tracks, turned on one of them, and gave him so great a blow with his straight sword that the one who received it did not want to pursue him any longer; and thus, on horseback, he threw to the ground up to three of them, badly wounded.

This was regarded by the French and others who heard of it as gallant behavior, in spite of the fact that the German's party were almost all killed or captured. Apparently so long as the enemy preserved a proper distance, whatever it was, one could leave an engagement without exactly running away from it— and hence preserve honor. Centuries earlier, in Stephen's time, the redoubtable and puzzling Earl of Gloucester behaved with exactly the same end in view: being attacked by a superior force,

28. Ibid.
29. Jordan of Fantosme, *Chronique,* ll. 750–51; *RS, 82:3,* 266.
30. Froissart, *Chroniques, 6,* 230–31.

and having gotten the empress safely away, "he himself rode slowly, to prevent his journey being thought like a flight,"[31] and was captured as a consequence. The distinction between running away and leaving the scene was critical to one's honor, although it must at times have been difficult to determine.

This concern for appearances could make medieval armies as skittish and unpredictable as elderly female relatives. On the ill-fated crusade of Richard the Lion-Hearted, according to Pierre de Langtoft, Richard and King Philip of France undertook separate military engagements prior to the assault on Acre. Richard rode heroically and invincibly against the infidel, while Philip had no success whatsoever in his attempt to take a minor outpost. When Philip heard that Richard was returning from his own expedition to help him, he is reported to have said,[32]

> We obtain no success;
> Let us return toward Acre, for it would be shame to us,
> If in our presence that castle be conquered
> By King Richard, and less would fear us
> The pagan, and Christians would honor us less.

Poor Philip. He had been urged to undertake the crusade in the first place because the reconquest of the Holy Land "would be a great honor,"[33] but every occasion for honor was also an occasion for dishonor and its concomitant, the scorn of enemies. The posture of honor and, presumably, the terror in the enemy breast, however, could be maintained after a fashion by simply leaving the scene.

This sort of moral crisis usually presented itself in the form of a military confrontation. To be caught in a military posture by an enemy of superior force was an awkward business. Thus were the disinherited lords of Scotland, when caught in such a fix, exhorted:[34]

> Let us think of our great privilege, to show that we are descended from good knights, and of the great honor and profit to which God has destined us, and of the great shame

31. William of Malmesbury, *Historia novella, NMC,* p. 66.
32. Pierre de Langtoft, *Chronicle, RS,* 47:2, 88–89.
33. Ibid., pp. 30–31.
34. *Scalacronica,* p. 160.

(*hount*) that will come upon us if, in this great business, we
do not show ourselves.

Pages and pages of medieval chronicles are devoted to the kinds
of shuffling—of challenges, of invitations to attack (or give up)
impregnable positions, and so forth—that the weaker party ordinarily resorted to in such situations. Some sort of face-saving truce
was usually the outcome.

The concern for public posture in military matters is revealed
by the fact that aristocratic chroniclers, and surely their audiences
as well, were much less interested in the actual fighting than in
the posturing that took place before and after the event.[35]

This can be seen in the account of the battle of Poitiers as reported in the *Life of the Black Prince*. The total account, from
the muster of the French host at Chartres, runs to about 700
lines.[36] Almost half of the account is taken up with preliminary
matters: the intercession of the Cardinal of Perigord is reported;
he tearfully appeals to each of the commanders in turn, and their
heroic replies are properly noted; the council between Edward
and John is then presented, with the parties speaking in turn;
the climax is the offer on the part of the French to fight 100
against 100 and the answer of the Earl of Warwick, concluding
with the defiance, "May God support the right, / Where He sees
it the better!"[37] (We have here, of course, another example of the
alternating narrative structure described in Chapter 2.) But even
then we are not ready for the battle; there follow about sixty lines
of noble speeches as King John addresses his army in general and
his marshals in particular. In other words, the first half of the
account is devoted to the noble postures of the leading figures in
the engagement.

35. See, for instance, the amusing recourse to literalism of the French
as reported by Froissart, 8, 276–79. They had besieged Brest and had
given the usual forty days for the city to seek relief before it surrendered.
A sea force of the English unexpectedly arrived within the specified time,
a force estimated to be stronger than the French, but lacking horses. The
French declared that they yearned for a fight, but it would have to be at
the point where the treaty of capitulation was entered upon, some distance
away. Since the English did not have horses this was impossible, and
after some more polite exchanges the French got off with the hostages
that had been given and their honor only slightly tarnished.

36. *Life of the Black Prince*, ll. 729–1400; pp. 22–41.

37. Ibid., ll. 890–918; pp. 26–27.

The actual fighting is reported in two different accounts, separated by the Prince's prayer when things are going badly. The first part of the first section illustrates the relatively minor interest in actual fighting during the Middle Ages:[38]

> Then began a confused shouting,
> The cries and the noise arose,
> And the armies began to approach.
> Then to thrust and to throw
> Both sides began;
> None of them held himself aloof.
> Lords, from what I heard,
> The good Earl of Salisbury
> Of the Prince had the rearguard,
> But that day, may God preserve me,
> He went to battle in the first ranks;
> For, full of anger and bad will
> The Marshal came upon him,
> Believe me, on foot and on horseback,
> And ran against him vigorously.
> When the Earl sees this force,
> He turns his battle toward them
> And in a high voice he shouts:
> "Forward, seigneurs, for the mercy of God,
> Since it pleased St. George that,
> While we were the last ones
> And we are now the very first,
> Let us so behave that we may have honor there."
> Then you should have seen the barons
> Getting ready to fight well:
> Great pleasure to look upon
> That who had no stake in it,
> But truly, it was a great pity
> And a marvelous and hard thing.
> There were many creatures
> Who on that day were put to their end.
> Archers were shooting by volleys
> More thick than flying rain—

38. Ibid., ll. 1157–1202; pp. 34–46.

> [The archers] who were on both sides,
> Besides the horses in armor.
> Finally you can see coming straight
> A courageous and valiant knight
> Who was called Guichard d'Angle;
> This knight would not place himself on the side,
> But in the middle of the melee he kept striking,
> Know it, with lance and sword
> And the Marshal of Clermont
> And Eustace of Ripemont
> And the good seigneurs of Aubegny,
> Each one did good fighting too.

Several peculiarities are to be noted about this passage. At least half of it is peripheral or irrelevant—the speech of the Earl of Salisbury, the author's comment, and the lords listed at the end. The action presented in the passage is generalized; we do not hear any particular noise, we are told that "cries and noise arose"; we do not realize imaginatively any actual conflict, we are told that the barons acquitted themselves well in battle. Only once in the passage do we approach specific action, when Guichard appears, but even that is immediately lost by generalizing: "He kept striking, / Know it, with lance and sword."

The author makes his intention and his interest in the battle clear when he says, "Then you should have seen the barons / Getting ready to fight well." His intention is to elevate the action, to make it more impressive, even though he may lose all sense of the concrete event. This intention is even more apparent in the lament about creatures brought to their end. Such laments are standard aristocratic rhetoric, and their utter insincerity is beyond dispute. At the council between John and Edward before this very battle, for instance, the French knight who proposed the battle of champions ended by exclaiming,[39]

> I believe that it will be for the best,
> And that God will be grateful to us,
> If the battle is avoided
> In which so many good men will die.

39. Ibid., ll. 901–04; p. 27.

The French had no intention of permitting the weaker English to avoid a battle. The function of the exclamation is to dramatize the solemnity and the honorific character of the occasion.

This attitude toward action is equally evident in the writings of Jordan of Fantosme. If one were to simply remove from his chronicle the quoted speeches, invariably assertions of stance, it would be cut in half. At the same time, his comparatively brief accounts of action and the character of these accounts make it apparent that he was not really interested in action for itself. Here, for instance, is his account of the Scottish siege of Carlisle:[40]

> Great was the noise at the beginning of the fight.
> The irons resound and the steels grate.
> Hardly any hauberks or helmets remained intact.
> That day those within were knights:
> With their swords they cause many shields to be pierced,
> A good number of them they leave scattered along the walls,
> Who had no leisure to get up again.
> From now on it belongs to those inside to help,
> To endure battle and to break the shields,
> To keep and to protect their barbican.
> Now no coward would be of use.
> At the gate there was a great crowd:
> On both sides was great fury.
> You could have seen there many bloody knights,
> Many good vassals in bad luck.
> The swords resound and are thrust everywhere.
> Robert of Vaus defended himself vigorously,
> The son of Odart was in no way behind him.
> For his lord he dared great boldness
> To resist so many people—
> Forty thousand, as Fantosme does not lie.

Here again are all of the characteristics of the aristocratic view of action. The account is thoroughly generalized; the reader sees not one blow. The saga-like irony ("Who had no leisure to get up again") and the ironic understatement ("No coward would be of use") interrupt the action to emphasize its awesomeness. The la-

40. Jordan, *Chronique*, ll. 648–68; *RS*, 82:3, 260.

ment which follows the above passage (not quoted) is particularly instructive since it is not, as one would expect, a lament for the slain but a lament for the sorrow of the Scottish King William, who got nowhere in his assault. It functioned exactly as did the lament in the *Life of the Black Prince:* to heighten the dignity of the enterprise in which the heroes were engaged.

In attempting to evaluate such passages, it is necessary to remember that medieval writers were seldom very successful in their efforts at description. Aristocratic writers (and clerks as well, for different reasons) seldom had an eye for characterizing detail, and this deficiency was compounded by an overwhelming impulse to indulge in quantitative comparisons, given a remarkable scene or personage, and thereby lose the experience entirely.[41] But to characterize medieval aristocratic literature in this way is not to explain it. The writer who habitually generalizes his descriptions is not interested in specific details; the writer who habitually approaches his subject in terms of its magnitude is interested in the magnitude rather than the subject itself. The aristocratic chronicler interrupted his generalized accounts of battles with speeches and laments because they added to the dignity of the occasion and, at second remove, to the dignity of the participants. It seems safe to conclude that the participants assembled in the first place to do battle for similar reasons.

Aristocratic romances very generally shared the chroniclers' attitudes toward warfare. In *Morte d'Arthur,* for instance, knights ride out to combat incessantly, but the combats themselves are habitually treated in a most perfunctory manner. A single instance must suffice, in Book III, when Sir Torre was challenged by the knight of the brachet and combat followed:[42]

Then Sir Torre arranged his shield and took his sword

41. This is, of course, merely another reflection of the aristocrat's habitual magnification in the interest of stance. Ladies had to be fairer than Helen for the same reason that battles had to be fell—to enhance the dignity of all concerned. See below, pp. 143–44, for a further discussion of this aristocratic attitude toward description.

42. *The Works of Sir Thomas Malory,* ed. Eugene Vinaver (3 vols. Oxford, Oxford University Press, 1947), *I,* 111. One would have expected Sir Torre to begin the fight with shield and lance, particularly since he apparently draws a second sword later. But I know of no instance in Middle English where "glayve" means anything but "sword."

[*glayve*] in his hands. And so they came fiercely together as though they were fresh men, and they drove both horses and men to the earth. Straightway they arose lightly and drew their swords as eagerly as lions, and they put their shields before them, and they smote through their shields, so that the little pieces fell on both sides. Also they hewed their helmets, so that the hot blood ran out, and the thick mail of their hauberks they chopped up and split in pieces, so that the hot blood ran to the earth. And they both had many wounds and were exceedingly weary.

But Sir Torre perceived that the other knight fainted, and then he followed after him quickly and redoubled his strokes, and struck him to earth on the one side.

This is a thoroughly generalized account; one need only compare it with the report of a boxing match in any modern newspaper—or with Homer—to see how far short it falls from being an account of action. This does not, of course, constitute a criticism of Malory; it only points out that Malory was interested in fierce fighters and not fights.

There is other more direct evidence of the fact that warfare was valued chiefly for the heroic stance it permitted. Jordan of Fantosme, for instance, began his *Chronicle* with an account of King Louis of France holding a council on the subject of war with England. King Louis[43]

> Held a great council of all his good friends.
> Of the old king of England he was so thoughtful
> That the gentle King Louis was near to going out of his mind.

"Gentle King Louis" was first comforted by the Count of Flanders in fairly moderate language, but the Count of Blois was a stranger to moderation:[44]

> Gentle King of St. Denis, rage possesses me in my body,
> I am your liege-man through faith and through homage,
> Ready am I to go fighting and find an host,
> Forty days will I serve you in the first rank,

43. Jordan, *Chronique*, ll. 32–35; *RS*, 82:3, 204.
44. Ibid., ll. 46–59; *RS*, 82:3, 206–08.

And I will do to King Henry, I believe, such damage
That he will not indeed be restored to his complete
    possessions.
He will not be cured, be it in the plain or the forest,
If he does not give back the inheritance to the young king,
    his son—
The Kingdom of England—if he wishes to do what is wise.
Leave to him Normandy, if your anger diminishes.
If there is in this proposal any error and I have said anything
    insulting
Of which anyone might accuse me in his own words,
Here am I in your court ready to offer my gage.
That person is faithless to you, so to seek your disgrace.

This is pure posturing, as was Henry II's reputed response, "Rage
seizes my body: I am nearly mad."[45] But the proper emotional
posture was very much a part of the meaning of an event and,
indeed, of life.

In the twelfth century, public passion was the mark of the
heroic life. Two hundred years later the fashion was different.
Here is a brief letter, attributed to the Bastard of Spain, written
upon learning that an invasion by the Black Prince was imminent:[46]

Very powerful and very honored
And noble princes of Aquitaine:
Dear sires, it is a sure thing,
According to what we have heard,
That you and your people have come
And have entered the harbors,
And that you have made an agreement
And you are allied
With our enemy
About which we are very surprised.
I do not know who counsels you so,
For never have I injured you,
Nor have I, in anything acted badly toward you,
For which you would be justified in hating us,

45. Ibid., l. 130; *RS*, 82:3, 214.
46. *Life of the Black Prince*, ll. 2404–35; p. 74.

Or be justified in taking
That little which God has given us
Of land by his will:
But because we know well
That there is no seigneur of lands
Or creature in this world
To whom God has given such fortune
In arms, as He has to you,
And we know well that you and all
Yours seek only, without fail,
To have a battle,
We amicably pray you
That you be willing only
To let us know through which part
You will enter our seigniory,
And we promise you
That we will go toward you
To give you battle.

Courtesy was the thing in the fourteenth century, but proper posture was still the essence of the matter. The King of Castile was behaving improperly, or at least missing an opportunity, when, upon hearing of the approach of John of Gaunt, he "became all pensive," and he "did not show, at these beginnings, all his courage [or spirit]."[47] On the other hand, the Black Prince did show his courage when he received the letter quoted above, but whereas Henry II was expected to rage, the Black Prince "manifested a very great joy."[48]

Stance for its own sake is everywhere apparent in the aristocratic life of the fourteenth century—in the gallant deeds done because of some gratuitous oath or another,[49] in the ladies sending off their knights to dangerous places in the interest of derring-do,[50] and most of all in the incredible pageantry which Froissart found

47. Froissart, *Chroniques*, *11*, 330.
48. *Life of the Black Prince*, l. 2442; p. 75.
49. As, for instance, the young men who wore patches on their eyes on the embassy to Valenciennes, quoted in Chapter 3, p. 85.
50. The *Scalacronica*, pp. 145–46, tells of a knight ordered by his lady to win distinction for a helmet she gave him by knightly activity in remote parts.

to be of such absorbing interest.[51] But the importance of stance
was nothing new. The twelfth century, too (and Beowulf, for
that matter), found that the correct posture was very nearly at
the heart of the aristocratic life. The essential difference is that
in the twelfth century the correct stance was still ordinarily attached to specific, and particularly central, relationships with
suzerain or enemy. By the last half of the fourteenth century,
posture had become generalized. When Sir Walter Manny asked
to be allowed to invade France first "and to make war there and
take some castle or strong town"[52] because he had promised some
lords and ladies that he would do so, his posture was directed to
the world in general and no one in particular. But a stance divorced from specific relationships can become simply silly, particularly if the hazards in that stance are systematically minimized.
This happened in the fifteenth century, if not earlier.

One other characteristic of the aristocratic idea of good needs
to be taken into consideration, even if briefly. I have argued that
honor, conceived of as a kind of public posture or stance, was the
central aristocratic concern. However, the most casual reader of
medieval literature sees that the aristocrat seldom pursued honor
unalloyed. The knights of the Middle Ages sought both honor and
profit. In the passage from Philippe de Navarre, *Les Quatre ages
de l'homme* referred to earlier (which has, I believe, no equivalent
in literature certainly associated with medieval England), Philippe
wrote,[53]

> In his youth a man should use without laziness or delay, his
> prowess, his valor, and the vigor of his body for the honor
> and profit of himself and his dependents; for he who passes
> his youth without exploit may have cause for great shame and
> grief. The young nobleman, knight, or man-at-arms should
> work to acquire honor, to be renowned for valor, and to have
> temporal possessions, riches, and heritages on which he can
> live honorably.

51. See, for instance, the entry of Queen Isabella of France into Paris,
to which Froissart devotes almost twenty pages in the modern text.
Froissart, *Chroniques*, 14, 525 ff.
52. Froissart, *Chroniques*, 2, 489.
53. Quoted by Painter, *William Marshal*, p. 30.

Obviously, Philippe saw the pursuit of honor and the pursuit of profit as by and large the same enterprise; there can be no doubt that Englishmen saw it in much the same way.

It hardly needs to be pointed out that the honor of a victory in battle almost invariably meant profit in ransom and booty; for the knight who particularly distinguished himself there might be access to those most valuable medieval possessions, wardships, heiresses, and reversions. Honor ordinarily presented itself to the medieval aristocrat handsomely adorned.

But profit also contributed to honor. In the first place, one's military opportunities depended to a considerable degree upon the state one was able to maintain. The aristocratic world reflected in the chronicles naturally enough fixed its sights upon the great; and greatness—then as now—was not utterly independent of income. Furthermore, the giving of gifts, as well as the receiving of them, was, in itself, an honorific activity. Ambroise's *L'Histoire de la guerre sainte* makes as much of Richard's distribution of goblets and so forth as it does of his prowess.[54] Conversely, any limitation upon largesse was a shame and a disgrace. Pierre de Langtoft asserted that illiberality alone had undone Edward II.[55] Earlier, Matthew Paris had described Henry III's restrictions upon hospitality as "inexcusable," "shamelessly turning aside from the footsteps of his fathers."[56] (The degree to which largesse maintained its traditional forms is surely remarkable; on the occasion of Henry's visit to Louis in 1254, the gifts he sent to the French nobles were "silver cups, gold brooches, silken belts"—just the sort of things that would have won the hearts of Beowulf's warriors.[57])

But profit was still more intimately connected to honor. Lesser folk than kings within the aristocracy were also expected to display in their manner of life whatever social value they alleged for themselves, and failure to maintain such a state was failure to maintain one's honor. Thus the knights who fought with the young King Henry were not merely ruined by the devastation

---

54. See, for example, ch. v; *Three Old French Chronicles of the Crusades*, pp. 13–14.
55. Langtoft, *Chronicle*, RS, 47:2, 293.
56. Matthew Paris, *Chronica majora*, RS, 57:5, 114.
57. Ibid., p. 479.

that Henry II inflicted upon their lands; they were "disgraced" by the impoverishment that it entailed.[58] At the end of the period, King Charles of France admonished three French squires who had arranged a tournament with the English to "guard well the honor of yourselves and of our realm; spare nothing in maintaining your estate."[59] The manner of life, as well as actions, might be honorable or dishonorable.

Of course, profit and honor did not always coincide; conflicts presented stresses and difficulties for the medieval aristocrat. The Gascons in the twelfth century and the Germans in the fourteenth both had the reputation of abusing prisoners in order to extract larger ransoms for them; this was dishonorable conduct in the interest of profit.[60] Many a commander in the Middle Ages must have found himself in the situation of the Souldich de l'Estrade, to whom substantial military advantage came through a treacherous murder. The Souldich criticized the murderer angrily, but he accepted the advantage thus gained:[61]

> You have murdered him, and know that, everything considered, if I did not see great profit for us in this action, I would have your head cut off, and body and head thrown into the moat; but, since it is done, it cannot be undone, yet it is shame to a noble man to have died in this way. And we shall have more blame than praise from it.

Of course, truces and other arrangements between enemies were always exceedingly ticklish matters. Profit might well dictate a course of action that honor might not. Medieval chronicles are full of the subterfuges men devised in order to have it both ways.

On the whole, however, one must be continually astonished in reading medieval literature by the degree to which conceptions of honor dominated aristocratic thought. Profit, from some source or another, was indispensable to the honorable life, and it behooved the aristocrat to take care of this matter. William the Marshal became a kind of holy fool of chivalry in the early part of his life because he seemed to be genuinely unaware of the

58. Ambroise, *L'Histoire*, ll. 2195–2201; *I*, p. 61.
59. Froissart, *Chroniques, 14*, 58.
60. *L'Histoire*, ll. 1717–24; *1*, 63–64. Froissart, *Chroniques, 13*, 103.
61. Froissart, *Chroniques, 9*, 75–76.

necessity for profit.[62] But in their thinking about the matter and to a surprising extent in their conduct, profit was subordinate, the sort of thing a gentleman took care of with his left hand, out of the public view. The best evidence of this attitude is of course the romances, whose function was to celebrate the ideal, to present the aristocratic attitude toward life unflawed by awkward facts. The heroes of the romances lived in a world in which riches could be given away endlessly, with no necessity for hard getting.[63] The hero of a romance, like the hero of a Henry James novel, was presumed to have "funds."

Perhaps the foregoing analysis of the aristocratic idea of a good life can best be summarized by a short passage illustrating the life of one of the very great heroes of the time, in one of his few seasons of peace. Of the Black Prince during his residence in Gascony as its lord, the herald of Sir John Chandos wrote,[64]

> The Prince, who was so gentle,
> Took with him his wife,
> Because he loved her so much.
> By his wife he had two children.
> In Gascony he reigned for seven years
> In joy, in peace and in delight—
> In this I do not lie to you—
> For all the princes and the barons
> From all the surrounding lands
> Came to him to do homage;
> A good seigneur, loyal and wise
> They held him, with one accord

---

62. This is particularly apparent in the account of the battle of Drincourt, where William fought heroically but neglected to capture the horses of his defeated enemies (ll. 827–1162). The scene following, when the Marshal, having lost his own horse is teased about his horse-lessness, is one of the few mildly comic scenes in aristocratic chronicles (ll. 1163–1302). *L'Histoire*, 1, 43–48. The incident is described by Professor Painter, *William Marshal*, pp. 22–23.

63. The best example of this characteristic of the heroes of the romances is, of course, Malory's *Morte d'Arthur*. There may be an exception or two in the Middle English romances, most of which, it seems to me, were written for middle-class, rather than aristocratic, audiences.

64. *Life of the Black Prince*, ll. 1596–1638; pp. 48–49.

And, if I may say so, properly,
For, since the time when God was born,
There were not held such beautiful entertainments
As he made, nor more honorable
Because every day he had at his table
More than eighty knights
And at least four times as many squires.
There they had jousts and pageants [or feasts]
In Angouleme and Bordeaux;
There dwelt all nobleness,
All joy and all delight,
Largesse, gentleness and honor,
And he was loved with a good love
By all his subjects and all his men,
Because he did for them much that was good.
Much they esteemed him and loved him,
Those who dwelt with him,
For largesse sustained him
And nobleness governed him,
Discretion, temperance and rectitude,
Reason and justice and moderation:
One could say with reason
That such a prince could not be found,
If one were to search all the world,
As it turns around.
His neighbors and his enemies
Had great fear of him,
Because so lofty was his courage
That he reigned all-powerful in everything,
So that one should never forget his deeds,
What he said or did.

All the aristocratic values are apparent in this passage: prowess, loyalty, courtesy, and liberality in superabundance. One sees them here as did the aristocrat, in an intensely public setting. The medieval aristocrat lived life in a goldfish bowl because the value of his every action depended upon an audience; the significance of an important event rested upon its being public because the essence of good was public stance.[65] The passage quoted puts particular emphasis on the great role that the Black Prince played in the world, but it takes only a little imagination (and some memory of manuscript illuminations) to see how the Black Prince at the same time provided appropriate and satisfying stances for everyone else in that magnificent entourage.[66]

Human Nature

The medieval aristocrat was not, it must be said again, a thoughtful person. He did not generalize much from his experience, and he surely did not worry about the nature of man. Hence, strictly speaking, it must be admitted that there was no aristocratic idea of human nature. What functioned in its place was the aristocratic idea of good. The medieval aristocrat was an actor, although he took the performance very seriously, and he perceived human beings in relation to his script.

It came to this: human beings were fully perceived only insofar as they fell within the aristocratic value system. Perhaps the best evidence for this fact is the character of aristocratic literature. Huizinga pointed out long ago that Froissart attributed the same

65. The end of this development was pageantry and ritual, and not drama, because of the very human impulse, manifested over the centuries, to minimize risk to life and limb. When there are no real moral issues drama requires at the very least that the life and health of the participants be at stake. But from the twelfth century, the element of the test was less and less in evidence, due to the developments in armor-plating and an increasing spirit of kindliness toward one's defeated enemies of rank. With these developments in medieval warfare, the central aristocratic concern became trivial pageantry. See the fifteenth-century *Pageant of the Birth, Life, and Death of Richard Beauchamp Earl of Warwick K. G.,* eds. Viscount Dillon and W. H. St. John Hope (London, Longmans, Green, 1914), for the end of chivalry—a series of fifty-three line drawings of the honorific moments which made up the life of the said Earl.

66. Throughout the Middle Ages a major problem of kings must have been the appropriate distribution of gifts and other kinds of honors. Jehan le Bel, as quoted by F. S. Shears, praised King Edward of England because "He has always accepted good counsel in his needs and listened to his people, knights and squires, and he has honoured all of them, according to their condition." F. S. Shears, *Froissart* (London, Routledge, 1930), p. 101.

virtues to everyone.[67] But so did every other medieval aristocratic writer. Six or eight adjectives and their contradictories repeated over and over sufficed to sum up human possibilities, and these adjectives were class-words. Men were valiant, courteous, prudent, and so forth, or they were cowardly, discourteous, and reckless. Women were beautiful, charming, and discreet, with no other possibilities being allowed for. The English aristocracy of the Middle Ages saw people in terms of these "stance" words, and this perception was necessarily at the expense of the broad range of human characteristics. Thus was aristocratic literature so overwhelmingly quantitative. Ladies were necessarily "fairer than Helen" and armies "fairer than any seen since the birth of Christ" because it was the dignity of the occasion, and not its unique character, that mattered. Chaucer's astonishing perception of human individuality, discovered in the act of parodying the aristocratic view of man,[68] had neither predecessors nor perceptive followers. Indeed, it can be argued that no one in the fifteenth century even understood him.[69]

67. J. Huizinga, *The Waning of the Middle Ages* (London, Edward Arnold, 1924), p. 272. The biographer of William the Marshal, writing about a man who, in his early life, seemed not to fully understand chivalric values, is something of an exception, although only insofar as William himself was concerned.

68. This has been obscured by the failure of literary critics to distinguish between aristocratic and clerical ways of thought in the Middle Ages. Thus it is an undergraduate commonplace that the Middle Ages dealt in types and superlatives. But typing is particularly characteristic of clerical thought, and the aristocracy ran to superlatives. Chaucer's indiscriminate use of superlatives was not Chaucer being medieval, but Chaucer being funny. The Miller, for instance, who "wolde have alwey the ram" was a parody of the medieval knight because he was looked at in a way formerly reserved to the upper classes. Chaucer used the language of the upper classes on distinctly inappropriate objects for the same effect. See E. T. Donaldson's "Idiom of Popular Poetry in the *Miller's Tale*," in W. K. Wimsatt, Jr., ed., *Explication as Criticism* (New York and London, Columbia University Press, 1963), pp. 27–51.

69. This has not, of course, been demonstrated. But the argument would go something like this. Fifteenth-century courtly love poetry was created on the model of the *Romaunt de la rose* and, particularly, the "Litera Troili" in *Troilus and Cressida*. (This point has been well made by Leonard Nathan, "Tradition and Newfangleness in Wyatt's 'They Fle from Me,'" *ELH, A Journal of English Literary History, 32* (1965),

That this narrowness was perceptual and not merely literary tradition is shown by the aristocratic attitude toward other classes. The aristocracy had effective working relationships with the lower classes; the medieval social fabric could not have endured so long (in spite of occasional objections, most notably in the Peasants' Revolt of 1381) without regular and accepted lines of communication. There is even a good deal of evidence that these relationships were mediated for the most part by law.[70] But working arrangements, lawful or not, tell us nothing about the social attitudes of the parties involved, nor can manorial records define for us the relationship of lord to peasant.[71] In short, the economic and judicial records of a particular period clarify the customary relationships between classes, but they tell us nothing about the feelings surrounding those relationships. They do not authorize us to assume that the lady of the manor habitually carried hot chicken broth through the driving rain to aged family retainers, as some scholars would like us to believe.

The best record that we have of the feeling that existed between the aristocracy and other classes in the Middle Ages is, again, the chronicles; because Froissart was uniquely able to report on the aristocratic point of view without himself assuming its posture,[72] his *Chronicles* are an invaluable source of information on the subject; his point of view is indirectly confirmed by the other aristocratic chroniclers.

The reader who is not hypnotized by Froissart's fluttering

---

pp. 1–8.) But the *Troilus* is full of deliberate romantic exaggeration, and the "Litera Troili" is not merely a bad poem but a deliberately bad one. The fifteenth century was hence engaged in writing solemn imitations of a joke.

70. George Homans may be right in thinking that the customary nature, particularly, of the peasant's work for his aristocratic superior mitigated against resentment of that work. But a customary, contractual relationship tells us nothing about the attitude of the contracting parties toward each other. George Homans, *English Villagers of the Thirteenth Century* (Cambridge, Mass., Harvard University Press, 1942), pp. 339–49.

71. May McKisack, for instance, argues against the notion of a generally oppressed peasantry. See "The Fourteenth Century, 1307–1399," *The Oxford History of England* (Oxford, The Clarendon Press, 1959), pp. 342–45. But can one argue from baronial records to baronial behavior?

72. See Chapter 3, p. 81.

pennons and gallant speeches must be appalled by the amount of casual bloodshed he records. A castle or city that did not immediately surrender itself to besiegers became a potentially fatal place for its nonaristocratic inhabitants. When the Scots took the castle of Edinburgh in 1340, almost all of the English garrison were put to the sword, except the governor and six esquires;[73] when the Earl of Hainault took the town of St. Amand, he ordered that no quarter be given, and "few escaped who were not killed or slain."[74] When the French took a small castle near Hennebon, "they put all to death, except the governor,"[75] and at the same castle, a short time later, the English under the gallant Sir Walter Manny "slew all within," except ten taken to mercy.[76] The *Chronicles* are casually peppered with such slaughters.

But this kind of behavior must be approached carefully. It strikes the modern reader as immensely cruel, but this is, I think, a misreading. Cruel the medieval aristocrat could be, as in the punishment sometimes inflicted upon traitors and notorious malefactors. But the instances above do not reflect cruelty, they reflect indifference. This is clearly shown by Froissart's account of a minor engagement during the siege of Rheims in 1360. While the siege was in progress, a body of knights left the main army in search of adventure. They came across "a handsome and strong castle" which looked like just the adventure they had in mind. After some gallant deeds, in which an English knight was killed, the castle was taken. The two knights in charge and some other squires and gentlemen were taken prisoner, "and the remainder they put entirely to the sword." Thereupon, the English destroyed the castle as much as they could (they didn't wish to keep it) and returned to the main army; "they reported to the king and his barons how they had behaved."[77] The prisoners put to the sword constitute the most minor kind of detail in the whole engagement, of no more consequence than the coat of arms of one of the defending knights described in the same passage: both were stage properties.

73. Froissart, *Chroniques*, 3, 244–45.
74. Ibid., p. 279.
75. Ibid., 4, 54.
76. Ibid., p. 57.
77. Froissart, *Chroniques*, 6, 238.

One cannot, of course, posit some sort of common human sympathy as innate in mankind and describe as pathological all behavior that does not manifest it. Indifference to, or positive pleasure in, the suffering of others is probably more characteristic of human beings than our modern revulsion against man's inhumanity to man, which has been a significant force in human history only since the eighteenth century.[78] But cruelty and indifference are no more innate human characteristics than kindness; both states have their origin in fundamental ways of perceiving and feeling. (Nor can one assume that there is one particular way of feeling or perceiving behind cruelty, kindness, or indifference.)

The medieval aristocrat was not indifferent to death; the elaborate obsequies of the wellborn are sufficient testimony to this fact; the *Life of the Black Prince* and *L'Histoire* add to the evidence.[79] The medieval aristocrat was, however, indifferent to the death of those outside his own honorific circle. All of this casual beheading and burning implies the absence of any perceived con-

---

78. History in this respect is frequently misread. We are appalled at the world wars, the concentration camps, and so forth that loom so large in modern history, and we are inclined to see in them the degradation of western civilization. But there is a very real confusion between intentions and the means available at a particular time to realize them. Certainly there has been more cruelty and bloodshed in the twentieth century than ever before, but it reflects technological progress—not spiritual failure. We were not intentionally more bloody in World War I than were the crusaders who took Jerusalem in 1099, nor, to take an extreme example, were Hitler's ovens more lethal *in intention* than the Inquisition's *auto-da-fé*. The twentieth century is simply more efficient.

The more important difference between medieval and modern is, as the text suggests, the widespread revulsion that wanton cruelty occasions today. The attitude of the Allies toward German civilians in 1945, for instance, was infinitely more humane than the crusaders' attitude toward the Saracens living in Jerusalem in 1099, or even than the medieval English attitude toward captured French civilians in the Hundred Years' War. The mere fact that we can be appalled at our behavior at times does us credit; revulsion at one's own cruelty is, historically, a rare and valuable phenomenon.

79. See the account of the death of the Black Prince, where

> Then each person with feelings weeps
> And they lament tenderly,
> All who were present there,
> Counts barons and bachelors.

Life of the Black Prince, ll. 4130–33; p. 128. *L'Histoire* records a comparable grief upon the death of its hero (ll. 18368–76; 2, 300–01).

nection with the victims. If a modern reader suffers with King Lear or Anne Frank or a condemned prisoner, he does so because he sees himself in some way related to the other person. If, on contemplating the execution of a criminal, he does not say with Huck Finn, "I might be a murderer myself some day," at least he recognizes in the criminal the same sort of human consciousness as is in himself. The medieval aristocrat's indifference toward people of other classes was possible because he did not recognize any such connection. To slay or to spare was equally a matter of custom or whim because the victims stood outside that circle of values defining human meaning and significance.[80] One's own soldiery was hardly of more consequence; if they were killed, as Denys Hay points out,[81] one was relieved of the obligation to pay their wages.

The amount of casual bloodshed in Froissart is due in part to the fact that so much of the *Chronicles* describes knights away from home. General bloodletting or burning in one's own country was prohibitively expensive because what one burned was a source of aristocratic revenue. Financial considerations, for instance, were explicitly the reason for the preternatural patience that king and barons manifested with regard to the rebellious citizens of Bristol.[82]

But knightly activities surely had repercussions on the lower orders, even in England; they simply were not worth the attention of the aristocratic chronicler. We know from other sources that the Scots border wars were exceedingly destructive and bloody affairs, but the *Scalacronicon* of Sir Thomas Gray, which has for its chief subject these wars, has practically nothing to say of their meaning for the non-noble population. Jordan of Fantosme, writing during the domestic broils occasioned by the rebellion of the young Prince Henry, notices the indiscriminate slaughter of the English

---

80. The future Henry IV was particularly given to mercy in such situations, according to Froissart's account, but sparing was hardly more noteworthy than general slaughter. For instance, Froissart reports of a certain conquered town that "Et se rendirent li demorans, hommes et femmes, à lui, et tous les rechut à merci, et respita par gentillèce le ville d'ardoir et de pillier" (Froissart, *Chroniques*, 5, 112). This is very casual language.

81. Denys Hay, "The Division of the Spoils of War in 14th Century England," *Transactions Royal Historical Society, 5th Series,* 4 (1954), 91.

82. *Vita Edwardi Secundi, NMC,* p. 72.

by the invading Scots, but only as a part of the grandeur of the occasion;[83] generally he is silent about those not of noble blood. During the campaign preceding Crécy, the Herald of Chandos reports that the Black Prince made a good beginning; "he overrode the countryside of Cotentin and wholly burnt and destroyed" a number of towns,[84] and the English, "to amuse themselves," put everything to fire and flame.[85] But even such bland notices as these are rarely found in aristocratic chronicles. When the French attacked Winchelsea in 1359, the clerical *Chronicon angliae* reports the indiscriminate slaughter of men, women, and children as well as the kidnapping of all women who appealed to the invaders;[86] the aristocratic *Scalacronicon* bypasses this aspect of the engagement entirely.[87] The victims stood outside the charmed circle of those whose fortunes interested the aristocracy.

This same herald reveals the aristocratic attitude toward other classes most clearly in his account of the massacre of Limoges, which shocked even Froissart:[88]

> But there they were all put to death or made prisoners
> By the noble prince of great renown,
> Which gave much joy around him
> To all those who were his friends;
> And his enemies had about it
> Great fear, and they were sorry
> That they had renewed the war
> Against him, you can trust me.

If the *Life of the Black Prince* were our only source, we would not know that there had been a massacre of 3,000 men, women, and children (by Froissart's figures[89]). The classes beyond the honorific world of the aristocracy had a shadowy existence for those who

83. Jordan, *Chronique*, ll. 631–37; p. 258, says: "Those who are caught in plain or wood / Will never tell their stories to any of their lineage." This is typical heroic elevation.

84. Ibid., ll. 169–73; p. 5.

85. Ibid., ll. 236–37; p. 7.

86. *Chronicon angliae, ab anno Domini 1328 usque ad annum 1388,* ed. Edward M. Thompson, *RS, 64,* 41.

87. *Scalacronica,* pp. 190–91.

88. Ibid., ll. 4049–56; p. 126.

89. Froissart, *Chroniques, 8,* 41.

lived happily within its confines. Churches, it would seem, were more real than people; at least their destruction occasioned more criticism.[90]

Some specific acts of mercy, again drawn from Froissart, perhaps contribute more to our understanding of the aristocratic view of human nature than the casual, class-determined view. In the massacre of Limoges, for instance, the French garrison, being surprised, gathered in one spot to give battle; three French knights especially distinguished themselves in individual action by their "many great passages of arms." The Black Prince, riding by, "looked on them with pleasure, and he repressed and softened his ill-will." These three knights, as a consequence, were allowed to surrender, and presumably lived to do more gallant deeds of arms.[91] In the midst of incredible carnage to which the Black Prince was apparently totally indifferent,[92] three knights by their honorable stance touched the Prince where mere suffering never could.

A similar response to courageous behavior occurred during the mopping-up operation against the Gascon and English free-booters, left over from the Hundred Years' War, who were ordinarily put to death when captured. But in the assault on a small castle, one of these freebooters, a Gascon squire, performed such wonders that the French knights cried out, according to Froissart, "Here is a squire of great courage, and whose arms well become him . . . It would be good to deal with him so that he may give

90. There are dozens of indications of this peculiar value judgment in the chronicles; see, for instance, Pierre de Langtoft's plea to the king for vengeance on the Scots (*Scalacronica*, p. 256):

> Edward, among all your reasons,
> Please think of the fires
> Of the temple of God Omnipotent,
> At Hexham, where that host
> Of the cross made roast,
> The figure of human salvation.

91. Froissart, *Chroniques, 8,* 42–43.

92. See Froissart's description: "There was there a very pitiful thing; because men, women and children threw themselves on their knees in front of the prince and cried: 'Mercy, gentle sire, mercy!' But he was so enflamed by anger that he cared not, and none of them, man or woman, was heard, but all were put to the sword, as many as one found and met, these men and women who were not at all guilty." Ibid., p. 41.

up the fortress and go elsewhere looking for his profit."[93] And so it was done. A similar motive was surely at work in a minor incident when Ventadour was recaptured from freebooters:[94]

> Messire William le Bouteiller found in the fortress of Ventadour a young squire from Brittany, a very handsome boy, whom they called "The Little Monk," who was a cousin of Geoffrey Black-Head [a notorious freebooter], and who had come here recently to learn the profession of arms, and had come out of a monastery in Brittany, for he did not want to be a monk. The French companions wanted to hang or behead him with the others, but the knight took pity on him and saved his life, provided that he would swear that he would serve him in everything that he wanted and would remain a good Frenchman, which he did.

In both of these incidents the leading figures were spared, in spite of their unsavory associations, by the relationship they bore to a compelling idea of good. This idea of good was not specifically moral, as the word would be used today; the good was a kind of public posture assumed in certain kinds of experiences.

In short, these specific attitudes permit us to conclude that during the Middle Ages the English aristocracy perceived the human world in terms of a code of behavior. What fell within that code was meaningful; human behavior that was not perceived in terms of this code hardly existed.

The modern reader may be tempted to see such a code as totally negative, to be particularly aware of what it excluded—undoubtedly a great deal. But chivalry as a way of thought did not merely exclude; it also functioned positively. It gave meaning to the behavior included within its narrow range, and hence it permitted a kind of communication. The people to whom the code applied understood each other in its light; the kind of reality they achieved for others, and probably for themselves, would have been impossible without the perceptual system. One can see this perhaps best of all in L'Histoire de Guillaume le Marechal. The chivalric code was an intermediary in all of William's relationships with his

93. Ibid., 9, 208.
94. Ibid., 14, 103–04.

contemporaries (as I have pointed out in connection with his behavior toward King John[95]), but the code itself was the basis for important kinds of communication.

At the same time, it must be acknowledged that this chivalric code was extremely limiting, and much of what we of the twentieth century value in human beings the medieval aristocrat simply did not perceive. The code was so limited, in fact, that its highest conceptions, the good and the noble, were in danger of being divorced entirely from the world of human beings. This possibility is most apparent when we consider how material objects assumed an honorific role—even a kind of honorific personality—in the chivalric mental world. We can pass by the Gringolets and Excaliburs and consider merely the peculiar attributions that the land itself might acquire. Two instances will serve to illustrate a general impulse toward anthropomorphism. Froissart quotes the Duke of Brittany as claiming that a whole series of legal privileges are based upon the fact that "the fief of the duchy of Brittany is of such a noble condition."[96] The nobles of Aquitaine argued in the same spirit against an abortive attempt to transfer the Duchy from the crown of England to the Duke of Lancaster:[97]

> and had it recorded that the city of Bordeaux, the city of Bayonne, the city of Dax, and all the seigneuries which touch them and belong to the territory limited by the boundaries of those cities, are of such a noble condition that no king of England, by whatever action he may take, can take them out of, or separate them from the domain of the crown of England.

The notion of the nobility of a region requires scrutiny, especially since we have inherited the terminology. This kind of language applied to territory at the present time—or at any time since the sixteenth century—would probably predicate for that territory the transcendence which was perhaps the most important legacy of Rome. When Shakespeare celebrated "this teeming womb of royal kings" in *Richard II*, England had already acquired from its

95. See above, p. 109.
96. Ibid., *14*, 364.
97. Ibid., *15*, 160.

classical educators the semidivine status which classical patriotism and modern nationalism presume.[98]

But such a status is clearly not the presumption underlying these passages from Froissart; aristocratic allegiance in the fourteenth century was still a contractual relationship between lord and vassal.[99] Froissart refers to pieces of property upon which the honorific character of their rulers has rubbed off. This fief and these cities have acquired a human quality, and hence they have also acquired something of a human personality. This can only happen when the feeling for human personality, as it might be perceived at any time since the sixteenth century, is very thin. The qualities of the chivalric knight, in short, were not personality traits, they were attributes, and one suspects that the knight himself might very easily get lost in them.[100]

Chivalry and Courtly Love

Chivalry was more than a code of behavior; it was also a kind of perceptual organization giving shape and meaning to the world in which the knight lived. It was inevitable that as women sought their own kind of meaning in the aristocratic world they found it in terms analogous to those of chivalry.

Even the most sympathetic medievalists are pained by the crass attitudes manifested toward wellborn women in the matter of marriages. It is difficult not to be critical of a society which habitually shipped off girls of fourteen or so, perhaps to another country, to be married to eligible males whom they had never seen. But one needs to remember that women were a part of this

98. Among the numerous discussions of this vexed question see especially Hans Baron, *The Crisis of the Early Italian Renaissance* (2 vols. Princeton, Princeton University Press, 1955), *1*, 38–120.

99. The Duchy of Brittany itself was the scene of protracted hostilities between the Duke and Oliver Clisson, for instance, and the other vassals flatly refused to aid the Duke; only feudal considerations were involved. Froissart, *Chroniques, 15,* 103–04.

100. One should perhaps call attention in this connection to the legal idea of *libertas* as a right which could adhere to a piece of property or an office as readily as to a human being, although I am not sure of its relationship to the subject under discussion. The classic study is of course that of Fritz Kern, *Kingship and Law in the Middle Ages,* Eng. trans. S. B. Chrimes (Oxford, Blackwell, 1939).

perceptual world too, and they shared its values. As men were concerned to improve their honorific status by marriage, so too, surely, were women. Thus in a very formal complaint attributed to the wife of the Black Prince as he set off to Spain, she is supposed to have said,[101]

> Alas! What would I do,
> God and love, if I were to lose
> The very flower of nobleness,
> The flower of very noble dignity,
> The one who has in the world no peer
> For valiance, to speak truly.

And the wife of the Spanish Bastard, whom the same prince had temporarily discomfited, lamented her lot in similar terms of the status she had received from her husband. She exclaimed, in an imaginary interview with the Black Prince,[102]

> Alas! Why was I born?
> I was queen of Castile,
> With a crown of rich and fine gold,
> But fortune did not last long.
> Alas! Death, you who are common to all,
> What do you wait for? I would like to die now,
> For never would I be able to have
> Pleasure or joy,
> Every time they will say,
> "Here is the Queen of Spain,
> Whom the Great Company crowned!"
> Alas! Prince, your power has made
> Me to fall from the heights to the depths.
> Much honored is the lady
> Who is destined to lie by you,
> Because one can rightly say that she has the flower
> Of the whole world and the best,
> And that she has mastery over all the world.

In these (idealized) passages, it is clear that aristocratic women understood life in terms similar to their masculine counterparts.

101. *Life of the Black Prince,* ll. 2057–62; p. 63.
102. Ibid., ll. 3576–93; p. 110.

For women as for men, this value system had both a positive and a negative function; it established a system of meanings within which relationships were possible, but that system sharply limited the appreciation of human variety, and the individual could easily be overlooked. The lady lamenting the possible loss of the Black Prince, for instance, was not thinking of a man named Edward to whom she was married.

But feminine attachment to chivalric values did not provide women with roles in the chivalric world; both ladies quoted above were simply reflections of their husbands' status. The role was provided by a parallel code of behavior known today as courtly love. Unfortunately, documents permitting us to understand courtly love do not appear in quantity in England until late in the fourteenth century, although the assumptions of courtly love were surely introduced into England by Eleanor, the memorable queen of Henry II. It seems most likely that courtly love was a viable English tradition from her time, but evidence is scarce.[103]

Courtly love attempted to give women an honorific role in society in two essentially different ways. First, it attempted to relate them meaningfully to warfare, the major preoccupation of chivalry. Even before Joan of Arc, an occasional woman had attempted to find a place in man's world directly, in armor plate or upon the castle battlements,[104] but this was not practical on a large scale. But the lady could, it was felt, be of some indirect consequence by inspiring her knight to outdo himself in chivalric enterprises. She might even win battles symbolically by virtue of her favor tacked onto the knight's helmet. This courtly game was of course the chief subject of the medieval romance. But it was not merely a figment of the romancer's imagination (or perhaps, in this instance, life followed fiction), although reflections of it are not common in the chronicles.[105] However, the romances themselves —the major statement of this element of courtly love—suggest

103. The evidence has been brought together by H. J. Chaytor, *The Troubadors and England* (Cambridge, England, Cambridge University Press, 1923), especially pp. 98–135.

104. Thus, the Countess of Montfort undertook to defend Brittany after the capture of the Count, and on at least one occasion rode up and down in armor soliciting enthusiasm from a besieged town. Froissart, *Chroniques*, 3, 421 ff.

105. See p. 85, for an example.

that this role could not have been very satisfactory to the women, since most of the time they were a mere excuse for the hero's usual hyperthyroid activity. And when Guinevere attempted to demonstrate her power by turning Lancelot's courage and prowess off and on, the whole relationship became absurd.[106] Even the aristocratic audience, it would seem, had little taste for such nonsense.[107]

Second, courtly love attempted to define an adequate social role by proposing attributes for the courtly lover, particularly the lady, and the proper relationship between lady and gentlemen—a relationship defined essentially in terms of stance. It was thus an extension of chivalry. The knight now had a role to play in hall as well as on horseback, and this role was particularly directed to women. In defining the woman's role, courtly love was clearly more successful.

The role of women was defined in terms of both physical attributes and proper behavior. But, as with chivalry, the terms used were so invariable that they were surely recognized as purely honorific; it would be a mistake to regard them as having much to do with reality. The "rollyng eyes whyche are as glasse clere," the "mowth as sweth as lycory," the brows that were "both brant & bright"—these attributions are as constant in substance as the epithets of *Beowulf,* and as little designed to particularize. They asserted the social status of the beloved, her place within the honorific world of the aristocracy.

The social and personal gifts of the lady were less important, apparently, since far less verbiage was devoted to them, but they were equally invariable. She was necessarily "gentyl," "curteysse," "demure," and, at least up to a point, "mercilesse." These specifications, like the parallel chivalric ones, had, by the late fourteenth century, become even more meaningless than the terms supposed to refer to physical attributes. "Pappes round as any ball" had a referent, whether or not the description was accurate, and hence

106. Chrétien de Troyes, *Le Chevalier de la charrette,* Eng. trans. W. Wistar Comfort, "Lancelot" in *Arthurian Romances* (London, Everyman's Library, 1914), pp. 270–359.

107. Vinaver points out that the story was radically changed by the first redactor fifty years later, and Lancelot's unnatural behavior was omitted in all subsequent treatments of the story. *The Works of Sir Thomas Malory* (Oxford, Oxford University Press, 1947), 3, 1579–81.

it retained some meaning. But the specifications of the spirit did not, and through years of use as quasi epithets they lost all meaning except the honorific implication which the user was chiefly concerned to exploit. The Middle English courtly lyric clearly reflects the end of such a process.

The lady's part in the chivalric play remained passive, even after the appearance of courtly love. This is apparent in the relatively little attention paid to the behavior expected of her. In the first part of the *Romance of the Rose,* for instance, the heroine (if she can be called that) is simply a beautiful object to be won in spite of social barriers; courtly lyrics reflect the same situation.

The real emphasis was upon the proper role of the aristocratic gentleman, and this was as invariable as the lady's charms. His was the posture of the defenseless suppliant. The chivalric analogy was not merely that of the noble and his sovereign, but of the noble who had been declared out of his sovereign's mercy and hence had neither the most elementary rights nor any proper status. The more sophisticated suppliant might imply, of course, that circumstances alter cases, and that the quality opposite to "mercilesse," "pitiful," had better be forthcoming in due time.[108] (It is interesting to note that when the paragons themselves took to verse, as they occasionally did, it was to assume exactly the same hopeless role.[109])

Although direct evidence is slight, it seems likely that the essentially sexual man–woman relationship of courtly love became, in fact, the paradigm relationship for aristocratic men and women generally. The aristocrat in the fourteenth century probably treated every woman of his class as though she were his only love (at least potentially), and the ladies also must have taken the same sort of public stance toward all gentlemen. At least this is what we observe later. As with chivalry, this generalizing of roles could only have limited genuine human relationships.

108. See, for instance, "A Lover's Plaint against Fortune," by William de la Pole, Duke of Suffolk, whose tone is utterly complacent amid the standard lamentation. Rossell Hope Robbins, ed., *Secular Lyrics of the XIVth and XVth Centuries* (2nd ed. Oxford, The Clarendon Press, 1952), pp. 185–86.

109. See "To her Lover" and "A Mocking Letter to Her Lover" for examples of this unusual reversal of roles. Ibid., pp. 218–20.

Courtly love (extended as it was in reality to include courtly behavior generally) was hence analogous to chivalry. Like chivalry it defined the good, and like chivalry it permitted a kind of human relationship. But it was like chivalry also in the fact that the relationship it proposed was narrow. W. H. T. Jackson has pointed out that in the courtly romances the emphasis was upon knightly service to the lady rather than upon "love as a passion."[110] This is surely right. In the courtly lyrics, on the other hand, the superficial emphasis is upon love as a passion, but the terms to express the passion were habitual, narrow, and ossified—the passion was clearly valued for itself. Both the service of the romances and the passion of the lyrics were simply prescribed public postures. They were functional, they created the possibility of certain human relationships by publicly defining them, and they gave aristocratic women a real, if limited, status in the aristocratic world.

The very question, What is the nature of man?, places one within a certain kind of generalizing perceptual framework which the modern world has inherited from the Greeks. The medieval aristocrat was in all essential respects outside that framework, and hence for him the question would have been a senseless one. But he had in its place something comparable, a conception of what one necessarily had to have and to do in order to be a man.

This implicit conception of man was immensely class conscious and immensely public. The medieval aristocrat had to be gifted with fairness and prowess, and he had to cultivate the proper attitudes toward others of his own class, defined by a rather vague series of virtues, such as courage, loyalty, largesse, and courtesy. These proper attitudes were in effect stances taken toward experience—the ultimate values of the medieval aristocratic world. They gave structure, organization, and, most of all, meaning to that experience.

Everything the aristocrat took seriously—even hunting—was organized as a series of stances. As women took an increasing part in formal aristocratic life, they, too, were defined by similar prescriptions. Finally, in the fifteenth century, even the central reality

110. W. H. T. Jackson, *The Literature of the Middle Ages* (New York, Columbia University Press, 1960), p. 96.

of chivalric life, war, was so enveloped in stance taking as to lose its heroic significance.

The function of these prescribed stances was to make certain kinds of experience meaningful and important. But the obverse consequence was to deprive of meaning the experiences and human beings ouside the prescribed stances. No system of values, of course, can include all possibilities; but the aristocratic system of values was at the same time a perceptual scheme, and for that reason it was both very rigid and very narrow—it gave meaning to life, but at the same time it immensely reduced life's possibilities.

It also made for peculiarly limited human relationships even within the aristocratic class. Froissart says of the death of Anne of Bohemia, Richard II's first wife,[111]

> By the death of the said Queen, the King and all who loved her, dames and damoiselles, were troubled and shocked with sadness. She was ensepulchered in a solemn and proper manner, and her obsequies were later conducted in a leisurely fashion; for the King of England wanted them to be held richly and powerfully, and one was sent to Flanders for wax in a great quantity and at a great cost to make with it tapers and torches, and on the day of the obsequies, there was an illumination such as had not been heard of, neither at the occasion of the death of the good Queen Philippa of Hainault, Queen of England, nor of any other Queen of England who had been before. And King Richard wanted it so because Queen Anne had been the daughter of the King of Bohemia, the Emperor of Rome and the King of Germany, and King Richard could not forget her, for he loved her much and had loved her always since as a young couple they had been married.

The relationship between Richard and Anne implied by this passage is intolerably ambiguous. Who was the object of all of this magnificent grief—Anne or the daughter of the King of Bohemia? Such ambiguity must have characterized all personal relationships in a chivalric society, where no distinction was possible between the actor and the role he acted.

111. Froissart, *Chroniques*, 15, 137.

CHAPTER 5

The Clerical View of Human Nature

The medieval clerk, unlike the medieval aristocrat, was interested in knowledge for its own sake. Of course, this was not the whole of his interest. He was also interested in knowledge as a means of power. The omnipresence of astrology is by itself sufficient to lay to rest the traditional notion that nature was first approached pragmatically by modern science.[1] It is true that medieval clerics were not always entirely comfortable in their pursuit of knowledge for its own sake; St. Augustine's use–enjoyment principle, by which only God might be pursued for His own sake,[2] was never renounced by medieval theology,[3] and hence we have more than one theoretical treatise which attempts to subordinate knowledge to the only possible end for human activity.[4] But a general interest

1. Even so excellent a study as E. A. Burtt's *The Metaphysical Foundations of Modern Physical Science* treats us to the spectacle of an expanding universe opening up men's minds to new thoughts (pp. 28–29).

2. Perhaps the fullest statement of this principle, by which God was to be enjoyed and everything else used to realize the enjoyment of God, is the first book of *De doctrina christiana* (see especially sect. 20). There are several texts; the Migne's *Patrologia latina* text is found in *MP, 34,* cols. 19–36.

3. It was, for instance, substantially accepted by St. Thomas in the *Summa theologica,* I–II, q. 11, a. 3, *Opera omnia* (2 vols. New York, Random House, 1948), *2,* 47–48. Perhaps its most important formulation was that by Peter Lombard in the first book of the *Sentences (Libri IV Sententiarum* [2nd ed. Quaracchi, Ex Typographia Collegii S. Bonaventurae, 1916], *1,* 15).

4. Perhaps most important is the *Dedascalium* of Hugh of St. Victor, in which he asserts that "omnium autem humanarum actionum seu studiorum quae sapientia moderantur, finis et intentio ad hoc spectare

in the world and its ways, merely for the sake of knowing, is manifest in practically all of the documents available to this study to establish the clerical view of the world.

Then, as now, man was very much a part of the known world; then, as now, the ways of knowing were numerous indeed. About one third of the whole of the *Speculum naturale* of Vincent of Beauvais, for instance, is devoted to man, approached from the physiological, psychological, metaphysical, and theological points of view. A comparable interest in man is manifested in every comprehensive work of the period.

But there is a puzzle in the medieval view of man, so assiduously pursued. The lengthy disquisitions in Vincent and elsewhere are theoretical; they are about man, not about men. When one turns to the chronicles, for instance, to see how the individual man was viewed in the concrete, lived reality, the amount of material tapers off astonishingly. Since the point of the medieval clerical chronicle was to understand important actions of specific human beings, one would assume that the clerical conception of the nature of man would be easy to see. But this is not the case. It is bewildering to observe how, in view of his interest in human action, the clerk paid so little attention to the characters and motives of the actors.

Here, for instance, is a typical piece of action reflecting the relationship between Edward I and Philip IV at the end of the thirteenth century:[5]

> English merchants, being injured by various perils in the sea, complained to the King of England about the loss of their goods, who sent Henry de Lacy, Count of Lincoln, to the King of France, asking him humbly that with the assent of himself, through the kings and their councils, something

---

debet: ut vel naturae nostrae reparatur, vel defectum quibus praesens subjacet vita, temperetur necessitas." Bk. 1, ch. vi; *Opera omnia, MP, 176,* col. 745. Bonaventura's *De reductione artium ad theologiam* (readily available in the *Sancti Bonaventurae tria opuscula* [Quaracchi, Ex Typographia Collegii S. Bonaventurae, 1938], pp. 365–86) has the same intention. I do not see how anybody could mistake the theoretical character of these works.

5. Nicholas Trivet, *De ordine frat. praedicatorum, annales,* ed. Thomas Hog (London, English Historical Society, 1845), pp. 325–26.

of a suitable remedy be provided speedily against this sort of maritime loss. But meantime, while the Count awaited an answer, a navy of two hundred and more Norman ships, come together that it might attack an enemy more powerfully and, being attacked, might repel more strongly, had set out against Gascony, resolving that whatever it came upon from the other side, it should easily have as booty and kill those opposing, and afterward it should turn back gloriously burdened with wine, as if the liberty of the sea had been ceded to it alone, was taken by sixty English ships and led to England, six weeks before the Vigil of Pentecost, with all the men who were in the ships drowned or killed except those who were barely able to save themselves by flying in small boats. A rumor of this deed having spread through France, it moved the King not so much with wonder as with violent indignation. Therefore ambassadors were appointed, who asked of the King of the English on the part of the King of the French, that he should without delay return the ships with their goods, which had been stolen away by his men and received in his kingdom, if he wished his business for the land of Gascony to be advanced favorably in the court of France. The King, deliberating on this order, having held a council, sent over Richard, Bishop of London, with other prudent men joined to him, to the King of the French and his council, with an answer of this sort: namely, since the King of England held his court subject to none, whoever felt themselves injured by men of his kingdom should come to his court, and with these injuries by them stated, the King will order quick justice done for them.

Here is very painstaking concern for situation—even to the councils to which both kings were obliged by feudal practice—but absolutely nothing about the human beings generating the action. This distribution of interest is characteristic of the medieval clerical chronicle from the beginning of the period to the end. Clerical chronicles invariably strike the modern reader by a kind of thinness, and it is caused by the lack of concern for character and motive. Matthew Paris' *Chronica majora,* for instance, is a long document covering a relatively short period of time. But its length results from its breadth; it includes information that a modern author would never think of putting together in the same book. Its treatment of that material is, on the other hand, invariably thin because the action with which the chronicle is concerned is either connected very crudely to human motive and character or connected not at all.

There are, of course, exceptions. Well over ninety per cent of the material in these chronicles bearing upon human action does not relate action to any perception of the actor. But this leaves a considerable amount proposing some relationship, at least indirectly. Furthermore, a great deal can be learned for the character sketches, particularly of kings, which are occasionally found in these chronicles and which seem to have been a part of the traditional rhetoric of the genre. There are also atypical chronicles, most notably those by William of Malmesbury (not included in this study[6]) and the *Vita Edwardi Secundi,* which bear a peculiar relationship to other clerical chronicles.[7] The striking fact about the English clerical chronicle is nevertheless its lack of interest in the individuals whose actions it reports. To understand the origin of this paradox of the concern for generalized knowledge that excludes great interest in knowledge of the human individual is to understand the clerical view of human nature.

Character Sketches and Character

Character sketches of notable people, particularly of kings, seem to have been regarded as an essential element of the chronicler's art, and they are a major clue to the clerical view of human nature. They tend to divide into two types. The first can be illustrated by Trivet's description of Edward I:[8]

> He was a man of most expert prudence in carrying on business, given to the practice of arms from adolescence, by which he acquired for himself in diverse regions that fame as a soldier in which he greatly exceeded the princes of

6. Because of his atypical approach to action; see above, p. 68 n. He was thoroughly involved, otherwise, in the contradictions implicit in the clerical view of man.

7. See above, pp. 94–97.

8. Trivet, *Annales,* pp. 281–82.

his time through the whole Christian world. He was of elegant form, and of great height, by which he towered above the common people by a full head. His hair at adolescence was almost silver, inclining to yellow, in youth shading off into blackness, and he was adorned in old age by gray hair growing white. His forehead was wide, and the rest of his face well-shaped, except that in the drooping eyelid of his left eye he resembled the appearance of his father. He had a lisping tongue, to which nevertheless a capable eloquence to persuade in matters of pleading was not lacking. The length of his arms in proportion to his flexible body was great; in which, for vigor, no sinews were more suitable to swordplay. His breast projected beyond his stomach, and the length of his leg made it impossible for the firmness of his seat to be weakened by the running and leaping of his noble horses.

When he was idle as to arms, he was addicted to hunting, as well of birds as of animals, and especially to deer, which he was accustomed to pursue on running horses and, having caught, to stab with a sword or hunting spear. It ought to be very well known how he was held in the protection of the most high God, not only as an adolescent . . . but also by the fortunate outcome of the various perils which he encountered many times. . . . There was in him a *magnificus animus,* impatient of injuries, driven to be forgetful of perils when he sought to be avenged, which nevertheless could be easily softened by the showing of humility.

The second type of character sketch is represented by a description of Henry II drawn from William of Newburgh:[9]

Truly, this same king was endowed, as is recognized, with many virtues which adorn a kingly person, and yet he was also guilty of certain vices which are especially unseemly to a Christian prince. Especially inclined to lust, he exceeded the conjugal measure, holding in this, indeed, to an ancestral custom; but nevertheless he yielded the palm to his grandfather in this kind of intemperance. The queen was used for

9. *Chronicles of the Reigns of Stephen,* 3, xxvi; *RS, 82:1,* 280–82.

a time sufficient for progeny, but with her ceasing to bear, he begot illegitimate offspring in pursuing pleasure. Loving the delights of hunting more than was just, as did his grandfather, nevertheless he was milder than his grandfather in punishing transgressors of laws enacted for wild beasts. For the earlier one, as is said in its place, wished there to be little or no difference in the public punishments of men-killers and beast-killers. The latter one, however, suppressed transgressors of this kind with custody in prison or exile for a time. He cherished more than was just a perfidious people, hateful to Christians, namely the usurious Jews, because of the advantageous rewards which he harvested from their usuries ... He was a little immoderate in seeking out money, but the badness of the time following, exceeding all limits, justified him in this matter, and shows that a decent limit was preserved by him; except that, when bishoprics were vacant, he wished them to remain vacant a long time, that he might lay hold of the goods provided, and brought into the treasury what ought rather to be applied to ecclesiastical uses ...

He had most famous sons by Queen Eleanor: but, as the preceding narrative has shown, this father was most unhappy in his most famous sons. This is believed to have happened deservedly by the judgment of God for two reasons [Queen's previous marriage with Louis of France].

Moreover, because, as I believe, he had not yet sufficiently bewailed the rigor of that most unhappy obstinacy which he maintained against the venerable archbishop Thomas, I think that the end of this prince was so miserable, so that as the Lord did not, with holy severity, spare him in this life, it is pious to believe that he prepared mercy for him in that other life. For he was in his high place most studious in watching over and cherishing the public peace, in carrying the sword.

The passage from Trivet is a peculiar one. The early descriptive part is obviously dependent upon medieval rhetorical models;[10]

---

10. The most important authority on the art of description in the Middle Ages was Matthew of Vendome. A difficulty arises because, as

at the same time, the description would seem to owe something to aristocratic modes of thought. In any case, it is apparent that Edward's character was in essence made up of qualities which might or might not require illustration by some anecdote (omitted in the quotation). Such a description implicitly assumes that the truth about an individual could be summarized by a series of adjectives. The lack of any organizational principle by which Edward's special standing with God might have been disengaged from his hunting and *magnificus animus,* for instance, is notable.

William of Newburgh's description, on the other hand, is perhaps more properly clerical in its aim at an ethical judgment of Henry II. His failings were not merely listed, they were evaluated by a comparison with the scandalous behavior of his grandfather (Henry I presumably), and the judicious analysis was further balanced by a list of Henry's benefactions (omitted in the quotation). Furthermore, William's analysis is different in kind from Trivet's. William was after typical actions and attitudes, not appearances.

But two common characteristics of the passages are more important than their differences and must be noted. First, both writers approached their respective kings entirely from the outside. We have noted that for Trivet the character (if not the description) of Edward I might ideally have been presented by a list of characterizing adjectives. The same is true of William's sketch of Henry, although it is less obvious because the adjectives would ultimately refer to characteristic actions. (William's superiority to other chroniclers describing people moralistically lies in the fact that his standard of evaluation was another human being and not a theoretical absolute.)

The second characteristic is more difficult to describe. For both writers the descriptions were on one plane. There is no sense of any more basic motives or attitudes underlying the qualities enumerated, nor do the qualities bear any meaningful relationship among

---

Matthew's own examples suggest, clerks were not particularly interested in physical appearance. (See his *Ars versificatoria* reprinted in Edmond Faral's *Les Arts poetiques du XXe et du XIIIe siècle* [Paris, Librairie Ancienne Édouard Champion, 1923], pp. 106–93, and the other rhetorical texts reprinted by Faral.) Yet the whole shape of the description suggests a relationship to the medieval rhetorical tradition.

themselves. Hence the persons described remain, for a modern reader, flat; we cannot understand Henry or Edward because there is nothing to unify the attributes of either man.

This characteristic of clerical chronicles can be clarified if we pay some attention to what is involved in the word "understand." Unfortunately, in modern English, it refers to several quite distinct mental processes. If someone should say, "Do you understand what I want you to do?" he would really mean, "Do you know the successive actions I want you to perform, in their proper order?" This is understanding of a very simple kind.

But when we say, "I understand" a human being or a theory of human behavior, we mean something quite different. We mean that we perceive the essential connections; we see the whole as some sort of pattern. Understanding in this sense always involves a dynamic mental activity because the essential relationships between the bare sense data are not to be found in experience. To understand in this sense is to construct; the mind must perceive relationships which it cannot experience directly.

"Understanding" when used in this way presupposes, also, a process of integration accomplished by the subordination of some parts to others. We understand a subject when we perceive the hierarchy of principles which is its structure. I might say, "No one can really understand Freudian psychology who does not perceive its essential dependence upon Darwinism." I would mean by such a statement that Darwinism is an essential part of the structure of Freudian thought. The implicit assumption would be that understanding is necessarily understanding of such structures. To understand a subject in this sense does not mean to know all about it; there may, in fact, be lots of Freudian principles of which I am unaware, for instance. But I understand it because I perceive it dynamically, as a system.[11]

"Understanding" applied to human beings obviously means much the same thing. When someone says, "I understand William Wordsworth," he really means (if he is using language accurately) "I perceive a kind of qualitative relationship between the important manifestations of the said Wordsworth, as found in his writings and in his life." But when we speak of human beings we can

11. I trust that my debt to R. G. Collingwood's *The Idea of History* (New York, Galaxy, 1956) is obvious in the above passage.

perhaps go further than we can with systems. When we speak of understanding a human being, perhaps we always refer, ultimately, to an intuited perception of the person's fundamental principles of action. These principles are perhaps adequately described as purposes. Hence, to say that we understand a human being is to say that we perceive the relationship that his most important human purposes bear to each other. Such purposes are not necessarily harmonious, of course; we frequently understand a human being or a character in a novel at the very moment when his purposes clash (perhaps we always do). At the same time, these purposes must, in the nature of the case, bear some sort of hierarchical relationship to each other, and we understand a human being by perceiving the relationship between his major purposes.

It is this sense of human purposes which is missing in English medieval chronicles throughout the Middle Ages. Trivet's passage gives no intimation of a hierarchy of deeper motives and values underlying the superficial characteristics of the description; these characteristics *were* Edward for the chronicler. But, perhaps less obviously, neither is there a hierarchy of purposes implicit in William's account of Henry II. William was interested in more important manifestations of human nature than was Trivet, but for both chroniclers human nature remained a collection of manifestations. The characteristics noted by the chroniclers are free floating; they do not spring from any sort of unifying ground. The medieval attitude toward human character is very nearly summed up in Matthew Paris' remark about a certain abbot, that "because certain vices are accustomed to be mixed with virtue," the abbot did a wicked thing.[12] Even moral qualities bore no relationship to each other. This is an omnipresent attitude; so far as I have observed, no exception exists in the whole range of English clerical chronicles.

Nor, I think, are clear-cut exceptions to be found elsewhere in English medieval literature, with the possible exception of Chaucer.[13] We occasionally find a kind of realistic vividness, as in the rustic characters of the *Second Shepherd's Play* and the Seven Deadly Sins of *Piers Plowman,* but whether details are realistic or

12. Matthew Paris, *Chronica majora,* RS, 57:5, 700.
13. See above, p. 131.

idealistic is not the question. Never do we get a sense of human identity, even in these works, because there is no suggestion of complex human purposes underlying either the character or the action.

Human character is also invariably missing in the scattered biographies of the period. We get a far sharper sense of St. Anselm, for instance, from his letters and meditations than we do from his biography, and the same situation obtains with respect to Ailred of Rievaulx.[14] Peter of Blois' dialogue between Henry II and the abbot of Bonneville permits Henry some vigorous language, but it finally comes to the confrontation of two abstract value systems.[15] Perhaps the best biography of an Englishman written in the Middle Ages, the biography of Samson at the center of Jocelin's *Chronicle,* is more or less an accident. The Abbot Samson was a mystery to his biographer, and virtually every page reflects Jocelin's puzzlement. He had no categories by which he might make the Abbot intelligible (surely because the Abbot was so thoroughly aristocratic in his attitude toward his "barony"),[16] and hence Jocelin could only write down what he observed, with occasional expressions of wonder. Even in this instance, where we have as good a firsthand account of an English medieval figure as is to be found, it must be noted that the Abbot lacks, by modern standards, any real dimensions of character. The deeply purposeful hero that Thomas Carlyle found in *The Chronicle of Brakelond* originated in Carlyle's necessities, not in the medieval text.

It is not even certain that the idea of biography as a literary genre having individual men for its subject matter was present to medieval clerks. Jocelin, after all, wrote a *Chronicle,* and other medieval documents which pass today for biographies are generally concerned with candidates for sainthood. Saints' lives were written in great plenty, of course. But these ordinarily manifest an interest in saintliness rather than saints; the way in which incidents passed

14. Both texts have been included in Nelson's Medieval Classics. Daniel's *Life of Ailred* (London, Thomas Nelson and Sons, 1950) has been edited by F. M. Powicke; Eadmer's *The Life of St. Anselm* (London, Thomas Nelson and Sons, 1962) by R. W. Southern.

15. Petrus Blesensis, *Dialogus inter regem Henricum II et abbatem Bonaevallensem,* in *Opera omnia, MP, 207,* cols. 975–88.

16. *The Chronicle of Jocelin of Brakelond,* ed. H. E. Butler, *NMC,* p. 63.

from one saint's life to another is only one indication of this generalized interest.[17]

The fact is, individuals could not be very interesting because there was no way, within the clerical conceptual framework, to comprehend them. Individuals were collections of qualities, and their actions arose from the collections, not from the total individuals. The medieval clerk manifested very little interest in individuals because in a sense they could not exist for him. This is the origin of that apparent contradiction pointed out at the beginning of the chapter, between an immense amount of material written about man as a species and the scanty observations made of man as an individual.

Medieval Scientism and Human Beings

The medieval clerk should have been able to describe a human being exhaustively by a list of adjectives specifying his qualities and actions, and these adjectives, having no common ground, would be more or less independent. Knowledge of an individual man in this view was a knowledge of attributes, precisely as with knowledge of natural objects (as has been shown in the first chapter of this study). Hence we observe again a peculiar kind of coherence in the thought of clerical writers. In the second chapter it was shown that the medieval clerk did not separate the actions of human beings and the action of objects of physical nature into different perceptual categories: both were essentially of the same nature. But, as we see here, neither did he have separate categories for the perception of things themselves—human beings and inanimate objects. The same categorical framework (which was a kind of unquestioned assumption about the nature of ultimate reality) governed his perception of the human as well as of the nonhuman object.

17. To a much greater degree than is ordinarily recognized, medieval saints were regarded simply as vehicles of God's power. A collection like the *Legenda Aurea* dramatizes this point of view by its convenient juxtaposition of late classical and medieval legends; late classical saints almost always chose their religious profession as adults; medieval saints almost always heralded their special status before birth or at least before the age of reason. Jacobus de Voragine, *The Golden Legend,* Eng. trans. G. Ryan and H. Ripperger (2 vols. London, Longmans, 1941).

Guiseppe Toffanin has argued that scholasticism was scientific in its orientation.[18] This is surely correct if we accept "scientific" to mean, "directed to the knowledge of classes of objects." But by this criterion medieval clerical thought as a whole was scientific. Indeed, its categorical frame of reference permitted satisfactory and meaningful comprehension only of such classes.

The large amount of material about man as a species, collected in the encyclopedias, connects medieval physical science with descriptions of the activities of men. Here, for instance, is a passage from Vincent of Beauvais upon the powers of the soul:[19]

> And the powers of the soul are distinguished from each other not through actions, as by cause, nor through organs, nor through objects. Nevertheless, knowledge of the distinction of powers is at times according to a difference of actions, as when the Philosopher says, that acts are preceded by potencies and objects by acts, according to the *rationem* of knowing. And certain powers differ in organ, in act, and in object. It happens to certain virtues, or powers, that they differ in organ. But of actions differing in strength or weakness, quickness or slowness, there is one power principally, but it happens to the one power that it may make its action stronger or weaker, at times according to what the action was, but at times according to the suitability or deficiency of the instrument, and at times according to an extrinsic obstacle; which things either add to or take away from, the working of the virtue.

In this passage, the powers of the soul are, in fact, separate entities, bearing no fundamental relationship to each other, in exactly the same way that the virtues of precious stones and planets were separate entities. Vincent explains the variety of effects that each power in itself may exhibit in exactly the same way that Albertus explained the variety of effects that one astrological power might manifest.

Vincent's encyclopedia is analytic and scientific, but the per-

18. Guiseppe Toffanin, *Storia dell'umanesimo* (Napoli, F. Perrella, n.d.), pp. 7–41. I find Toffanin's reasons for distinguishing Thomism from the scientific character of the thirteenth century obscure.

19. *Speculum naturale*, 24, ii; *1*, col. 1710.

ceptual framework did not change when man was viewed as an entity. Here is Bartholomaeus' approach to a more popular subject, the ages of man:[20]

> Hence the age of man, according to Remigius, is nothing other than the relationship (*tenor*) of natural powers considered according to contrary motions or an intermediate quiet. And according to this, man passes and moves and never remains in the same state. Or according to Isidore, age is the space of life of an animal beginning from the conception of the foetus to the failing or ceasing after senility. And there are many diversities of age, according to Constantine and Isidore. The first infancy is generative of teeth, namely, the age newly born, which lasts seven months: which is to this point exceedingly tender and flexible and flowing, and spongy, for which reason it requires continual cherishing. And infancy with respect to the generation of teeth lasts for seven years. And it is called *infans* as if "not speaking," in that it is not able to speak nor to shape a word, with teeth not yet well disposed, as Isidore says. To which succeeds childhood, which is extended to the second seven-year period, namely, to fourteen years.

Here one observes again the peculiar relationship between word and object. Words are treated as if they had some sort of independent status in the nature of things, so that ultimate reality might be approached through the names given to objects. But this attitude toward words presumes a comparable attitude toward things, which must also have some sort of ultimate, almost metaphysical, existence. This attitude is manifested in the above passage as regards human states, which must consequently have a kind of real existence simply because they have names. The ages of man are not, according to Bartholomaeus, stages of human growth; they are a series of states, each absolutely distinct from what precedes and what follows it.

In short, man as a natural object was in all essential respects like other natural objects, according to the encyclopedists of the Middle

20. *Bartholomaeus de proprietatibus rerum* (Nuremburg, J. Koburger, 1519), Bk. 6, ch. i, f. viii.

Ages (and the scientists upon whom they drew). He was a collection of quasi-independent powers and states, and he might be known by an examination of these powers and states. But this view of man the species, because it does not envisage the possibility of any coherence in human character or behavior, denies the individual interest and significance. Medieval science thus provides an explanation for the lack of interest in individual men that clerical chronicles habitually manifest.

The Motivation for Human Action

If human beings were not intrinsically interesting to the clerical chronicler, then questions of motive also had no great importance. As a consequence, one can search through scores of pages of medieval chronicles without finding any interest in motivation at all. The clerical chronicler was interested in what happened; to this end it was sufficient simply to specify the actor.

But there are passages in which the chronicler speaks of the motive of his actors. These passages typically occur when there was felt to be some kind of problem about the relationship between the actor and his actions. Here, for example, is Matthew Paris' account of Henry III's machinations against the purity of the English nobility:[21]

> Also in the same year, the persuasive supplanter of the natives of England, wishing that all the nobles of his kingdom should degenerate, and thus that he might destroy the whole legitimate stock of the English to their destruction, and that he might disorder their noble blood with the melancholic dregs of foreigners, sorrowed that only Richard, the Earl of Gloucester, and his offspring were not contaminated by the sulphurous source. For the Earl was young, elegant, eloquent, prudent, and skilled in the law of the land, and such [a man] in all things that the hope of the nobles of England was placed rightly in his bosom, and he possessed the favor and grace of all. But the hope thus conceived deceived all; for an ignoble avarice, hiding for a long time, which thus broke forth in public, enormously darkened his nobility. Hence the

21. Matthew Paris, *Chronica majora*, RS, 57:5, 363–64.

> Lord King, smelling out his cupidity [proposed a marriage
> between the Earl's eldest son and his own niece, a foreigner]
> ... Urged on, then, by avarice, which alone among all vices
> is asserted to be a servant of idols, the Earl, exceedingly de-
> generate in this, and declining from ancestral nobility,
> consented.

The problem was that Matthew, at least for the time being,
thought well of the Earl of Gloucester. How then could the Earl
have consented to so monstrous a marriage? In resolving this
difficulty Matthew reveals a further relationship between men and
objects as the medieval clerk perceived them.

It will be remembered that the medieval clerk always regarded
physical action as presuming an object from which it originated.
But at the same time, that action was always distinct from the object, inherent in it, but not comprehensively expressive of it. A
characteristic action was in fact a kind of attribute. The virtue by
which a precious stone might have medicinal effects, for instance,
was not comprehensively expressive of the stone; it simply inhered
in it. The virtue might be lost and subsequently regained without
any other change in the stone. The fundamental discontinuity between an object and a particular action might of course obtain
between different actions.

Confronted with the spectacle of a good earl doing a bad thing,
Matthew did just what a medieval scientist would have done. He
proposed a new attribute for the earl, avarice, heretofore hidden,
but now open for all to see. The untoward action is then attached to
the new attribute and thereby explained. What might trouble a
modern reader, the absolute discontinuity between this new attribute and the old ones, troubled Matthew not at all. He already
knew, although he seldom bothered to say so, that attributes, not
men, caused actions.

This way of looking at experience is even more striking in those
instances when the relationship between action and motive was
obscure to the chronicler. John of Salisbury and Matthew Paris
were particularly apt to find such obscurities. For instance, when
John described the attempted resignation of the bishop of Beauvais, he confessed that he did not know whether this was due to
"lightness of mind, or fervor of religious zeal, or knowledge of

his own limitations."[22] Similarly, Matthew Paris did not know whether the Greeks refused to submit to the Roman Church because they feared its tyranny and avarice, or because they were contumacious.[23] Why not both? Because an action was the product of an attribute, not a human characteristic.

It is perhaps worth noting that this attitude toward action and character was entirely consonant with Augustinian realism. The logical outcome of such realism is to deny human character altogether; if justice, truth, memory, and so forth are themselves things of which the individual merely partakes imperfectly, then the individual himself is nothing but a pale ground in which these real qualities inhere. It was medieval realism, surely, that was responsible for the endless cataloging of vices and virtues—which was itself an attempt to put in some definitive fashion all of the adjectives which defined the actions of man.[24] But this cataloging activity was perfectly consonant with the chronicler's perception of man and his actions because neither the philosophical realist nor the scientist presumed any significant integration of human qualities.

The Perception of Man and its Relation to Experience

In the course of this study, I have several times pointed out an important limitation, that our documents only permit us to talk about how medieval people saw their world and do not ordinarily enable us to talk about the kind of people they were. Medievalists generally assume, I think, that medieval people were, in fact, pretty much like ourselves. I do not think that this was the case, but it cannot be shown that aristocratic modes of perception governed behavior. The medieval aristocrat, for instance, may have felt rather as we do even while he perceived other aristocrats in radically different terms.

22. John of Salisbury, *Historia pontificalis*, ed. Marjorie Chibnall, *NMC*, p. 70.

23. *Chronica majora*, RS, 57:3, 469.

24. The *Somme le roi* is perhaps the best exemplar of what was nearly a medieval genre; in the modern edition of the fourteenth-century translation it runs to more than 300 pages. W. Nelson Francis, ed., *The Book of Vices and Virtues*, EETS, no. 217 (London, Oxford University Press, 1942).

It can be shown, however, that the medieval clerk's perception of human behavior was reflected in his own behavior. His mode of perception did not provide any criterion of coherence, since it did not provide for human personality as we know it. The same lack of coherence is apparent in medieval clerical life. Medieval documents abound with evidence that at least a majority of clerks lived a radically incoherent life.

Let us begin by noticing the range of value judgments expressed by almost every important English chronicler.[25] Here, for example, is the wholehearted praise bestowed by Giraldus Cambrensis upon Richard I:[26]

> Among the virtues, therefore, by which he excelled (by a certain unique distinction), three remarkable ones render him incomparably illustrious: great vigorousness and high-spiritedness, immense gift-giving and almsgiving, always praiseworthy in a prince and adorning other virtues, and a firm constancy in mind as well as in word.

Similarly, Giraldus praised Richard's elder brother, Prince Henry, for being "more fierce by far than any beast" in the proper circumstances.[27] In both passages the point of view is manifestly aristocratic; when Giraldus wrote of the aristocratic world, he automatically assumed the prevailing conception of good, even though the bulk of his work was clerical in subject matter and markedly ascetic.

Similarly, the *Opus chronicorum* praised Edward I to the skies. His greatness was particularly manifested by the awe in which other kings held him and by his disposal of the kingdom of Scotland at his pleasure, with the remark, "It is more glorious to make a king than to be a king."[28] Henry of Huntingdon,

---

25. The two most important exceptions are Jocelin of Brakelond's *Chronicle,* discussed below, and John of Salisbury's *Historia pontificalis.* It is a part of John's real, though limited, humanism that he saw the kind of values implied in aristocratic thought and clerical disputes over precedence. This is most apparent, it seems to me, in his letters. The *Gesta Stephani* is perhaps a partial exception.

26. Cambrensis, *De instructione principum,* Dist. III, ch. viii; *Opera omnia,* ed. George F. Warner, *RS, 21:8,* 247.

27. Ibid., Dist. II, ch. ix; *RS, 21:8,* 174.

28. *Opus chronicorum,* in *Saint Alban's Chronicle, RS, 28:3,* 47.

writing during the Anarchy, praised a foreign noble, William of Normandy, for his warlike behavior; he even included a small poem as an obituary.[29] Even more interesting and instructive, perhaps, was the comment of William of Newburgh on the conclusion of one phase of Henry II's eternal conflict with Louis of France:[30]

> Of a truth, as we have heard, the King of France did nothing memorable in this war, but the favor of a joyful fortune smiled upon the King of the English. Indeed, through a hired soldiery, whom they call "Rutae," he stormed and captured Issoudun, with some other fortresses, and enlarged notably his borders into the province of Berri, thus compensating for his losses in Normandy.

This is a thoroughly secular judgment; particularly secular is that phrase, "nothing memorable." Yet two chapters later William attributed the renewal of the war to "the devil instigating."[31]

The text of Matthew Paris abounds with judgments from an essentially aristocratic point of view. When, in the course of a war with France, the Poitevins suggested to Henry III that he bring money rather than soldiers, Matthew observed with great indignation that they were treating the King of England as though he were "a moneychanger, a banker, or a peddler, rather than a king and leader of knights and magnificent preceptor."[32] In a similar vein, some nobles who stayed in France with Henry after his defeat were described as "lazily and shamefully frittering away their time."[33] The same Henry, being defeated by the Welsh, was an *inglorius rex,* and his accustomed pomp was a matter for contempt.[34] Dozens of similar judgments, reflecting an aristocratic estimate of some action or another, appear in the *Chronica majora,* and the knights who are noted in passing to be "of illustrious race, and renowned in feats of arms," or possessing other knightly virtues, are almost without number.

29. Henry of Huntington, *Historia anglorum, RS,* 74, 249–50.
30. William of Parvi, *Historia,* 5, xv; *RS,* 82:2, 456.
31. Ibid., 5, xvii; *RS,* 82:2, 460.
32. Matthew Paris, *Chronica majora, RS,* 57:4, 191.
33. Ibid., *RS,* 57:4, 231.
34. Ibid., *RS,* 57:5, 651.

From one point of view, this penetration of the aristocratic system of values into clerical chronicles is not surprising. As I have argued in an earlier chapter, the interests of the chronicler determined what was included in clerical chronicles. The mere fact that so many were chiefly concerned with secular activities is sufficient evidence that the clerk found meaning in such activities and that he shared to some degree the values implicit in that meaning.

Of course not all clerical chronicles reflect such secular interest. Aside from the numerous monastic chronicles of interest today only to county historians because of their lack of concern for national affairs, there is the *Chronicle* of Jocelin of Brakelond, which has almost nothing to report of matters not directly affecting the monastery. But it is also apparent in many passages of Jocelin —a good example is the judicial duel he mentions in passing—[35] that aristocratic activities were simply meaningless for him.

From another point of view, the secular judgments so common in most clerical chronicles are surprising indeed. Not only were the activities upon which the aristocrat put the highest value well beyond the range of conduct permitted by even the most charitable religious definition of acceptable conduct,[36] but the aristocratic conception of man stood at the opposite pole from the religious view and its implications. The aristocratic ideal demanded of its servants an aggressive attitude toward experience: honor and the honorable station in life attendant upon possessions were to be wrested from daily experience in the world. In his pursuit of confrontation and assertion, the aristocrat was engaged in an attempt to maximize the self, egoistically conceived. His notorious love of splendid possessions and pageantry reflected the same conception of achievement and virtue.

35. Jocelin, *Chronicle,* pp. 68–71.
36. The obvious intention of the documents which in sum spell out religious chivalry (see Chapter 4, p. 107), most notably Lull's *Le Libro del ordo de cauayleria,* was to bring aristocratic behavior into a relationship with religious doctrine. There is no evidence that any considerable number of knights ever took seriously its minimum requirement: that bloodshed have some point besides self-aggrandizement. *Le Libro* was translated by Wm. Caxton as *The Book of the Ordre of Chyvalry,* ed. Alfred P. Byles, *EETS, OS,* no. 168 (London, Oxford University Press, 1926).

When the clerical chronicler accepted, even for the moment, the values of aristocratic society, he necessarily accepted the attitude toward experience they implied. Yet he was also capable of entering sympathetically into the world of asceticism to which he was professionally allied—the world of hermits, devout monks, and hairshirted bishops. This was the world of medieval Augustinianism (and the concrete, lived religious tradition in England remained Augustinian to the end of the period).[37] In medieval homiletics the ultimate good was always "purity" or "innocence," and vice was habitually described as a "stain" or "wound."[38] This language is thoroughly antiexperiential. The good is something given in the sacrament of baptism prior to the self and to all experience in the world. A human being, in this view, is not realized through human experience; he is only marred by it.[39] So profound was this feeling that the seven virtues always occupied a rather minor place in medieval homiletics, and they were ordinarily treated as "remedies" for the vices, or as medicines by which the human soul might again approach the pristine innocence conferred by baptism and more or less inevitably lost thereafter in one's dealings with the world.

In short, medieval religious morality proposed a view of man

37. Modern interest in scholasticism has in some degree obscured this truism, which any fourteenth-century collection of religious documents will instantly demonstrate. Medieval ethical theory took its definitive shape in the eleventh and twelfth centuries, not the thirteenth, and the last great authority on the practical ethical matter of getting to heaven was St. Bernard. In over one hundred sermons, for instance, Thomas Brinton, fourteenth-century bishop of Rochester, quotes no one as an authority on the Good later than the Saint of Clairvaux. Sister Mary Aquinas Devlin, ed., *The Sermons of Thomas Brinton,* Camden Third Series, 85 (2 vols. Royal Historical Society, 1954). The University Sermons (nos. 39–42) in Ms. Royal 18B quote Grosseteste and Bonaventura, but the doctrine is essentially that of Bernard. Woodburn O. Ross, ed., *Middle English Sermons, EETS,* no. 209 (London, Oxford University Press, 1940), pp. 220–84.

38. The beginning of the pseudo-Augustinian *De vera et falsa poenitentia* runs through a traditional range of metaphors: penance "heals languors, cures leprosies, raises the dead, increases the health which it preserves; it restores the power of walking to the lame, fullness to the withered, sight to the blind." *De vera et falsa poenitentia liber unus,* ch. i; *MP, 40,* col. 1113.

39. Hence the common assumption, in the early Middle Ages, that salvation was virtually impossible outside the monastery.

as remote from the aristocratic as could be; there was no conceivable nexus between the two. And yet both conceptions sit
side by side in clerical chronicles. Saints and barons were equally
worthy of admiration to the chronicler who recorded their achievements according to the respective religious and aristocratic value
systems.

Nor was this receptivity to contradictory views of man a proto-
Chestertonian geniality embracing all things medieval. The contradiction was lived by many, if not by most, clerks in the disparity between their religious profession and worldly pomp.[40]
Of course this contradiction was in part simply the consequence of
permitting laymen, in all but name, to succeed to even the highest
ecclesiastical offices. Such offices were invariably treated as secular,
even when their possessors observed such minimum religious re-
quirements as continence. When Walter of Cantaloupe protested
against the Lateran decree concerning pluralism, he said:[41]

> Holy father, since many nobles, whose blood is the same as
> ours, hold many benefices, have never yet received dispensa-
> tions, of whom some are of advanced age and have lived to
> the present time honorably, and in extending hospitality as
> far as they were able have given alms with open doors, it
> would be exceedingly hard to be despoiled of their benefices
> and driven into ignominious poverty.

The language is entirely secular. Poverty was never, theoretically,
ignominious for a person in orders, secular or religious. Even the
virtues Walter claimed for his pluralists are essentially secular—
honorable living, hospitality, and almsgiving.[42] Walter spoke for
secular men; their religious profession was accidental in the Mod-

---

40. The late George Coulton has often called attention to what he has
labeled "medieval Puritanism," which in fact was generally a protest
against the intrusion of aristocratic values in ecclesiastical life. See, for
instance, his *Art and the Reformation* (Oxford, Oxford University Press,
1928), pp. 371–87.

41. Matthew Paris, *Chronica majora, RS, 57:3,* 418.

42. Although almsgiving was religious in origin, this double obligation to give is habitually recognized in aristocratic documents. Does not
the traditional monastic distinction between travelers entertained by the
abbot and those fed and lodged out of general funds reflect, perhaps, the
aristocratic distinction between the honorific largesse and almsgiving?

ern as well as in the medieval sense. Appropriately, he ended his protest with the suggestion that the legate thus addressed consult "his own safety" before deciding so momentous a question.

But it is also apparent that many earnest men lived by values which appear today as absolutely dichotomous, oscillating daily between private penance on the one hand and public pomp and display on the other. The most famous example of this double life is, of course, Thomas à Becket. Clerical pomp was at times attacked during the Middle Ages,[43] and it was defended in scholastic fashion by a distribution of the contradictory terms—the pomp to the office; the penance to the man. But the quarrels about various forms of pomp (particularly precedence) which litter medieval documents show that most clerks regarded their dignities aristocratically—they constituted a positive obligation.

How deeply aristocratic considerations of dignity penetrated clerical thought is shown most clearly in the *Chronicle* of Jocelin, written, as I have suggested before, by a most unworldly monk. The secular world beyond the walls of his monastery passed by Jocelin like a dream; nothing in the larger world interested him at all. Yet his chronicle is filled with quarrels and crises in which considerations of dignity and disgrace were paramount. One of Abbot Samson's first acts was to order his servants to provide "fittingly" for hospitality, that "he might not be disgraced by avarice in food or drink."[44] When a quarrel arose between some merchants and the abbey about tolls, it was finally agreed that the toll should be paid and immediately returned. Although Jocelin saw this as a means of preserving the liberties of both parties, it was clearly designed to save appearances; the abbey had instituted a toll which it could not collect.[45] As happened very frequently during the Middle Ages, the archbishop of the time, Hubert Walter, avoided visiting the monastery when his status was ambiguous for fear of the disgrace of being denied admittance.[46] When the abbot appointed a clerk to supervise some

43. Among the chronicles which are the chief materials for this study, for instance, we find William of Newburgh criticizing the dispute between the archbishops of York and Canterbury about precedence as a *vana contentio. Historia rerum anglicarum*, 5, xii; *RS, 82:2,* 444.

44. Jocelin, *Chronicle*, p. 26.

45. Ibid., p. 76.

46. Ibid., pp. 82–85.

badly run monastic offices, the whole monastery, it would seem, quivered under the ignominy and disgrace.[47] To the otherwise unworldly Jocelin these considerations seemed unremarkable if not inevitable, although it is perfectly obvious to a modern reader that they are a reflection of the ethics of the aristocratic world.

At least a majority of medieval clerks manifested an extraordinary tolerance of contradictory value systems. Contempt of the world was seldom challenged even obliquely by clerks; on the other hand these clerks paid the world its due, passionately in many cases, with no indication of any felt discontinuity of conduct.

The difference between medieval clerk and educated modern man is of course in part one of degree; we have not found the perfectly consistent human being. But there is also a difference in kind. Modern inconsistencies are apt to be found between theory and practice (which is perhaps ultimately between affirmed, conscious pseudo belief and real, although unformulated belief). But the profession of beliefs is apt to be relatively coherent. The important discontinuity in the value system of the medieval cleric was within the profession itself, between two absolutely unreconcilable views of life which were equally cherished and equally believed.

I would argue that this discontinuity was a result of the clerical perception of human nature. Given a view of man as a bundle of qualities, the clerk saw one action as a manifestation of one quality, another as a manifestation of a different quality. As a consequence, he behaved in a fashion that seems today highly discontinuous. To put it another way, our own postrenaissance views of human nature not only give us a particular way of understanding other human beings, they provide us with a perspective upon ourselves that makes possible a judgment of consistency or inconsistency. Clerical modes of perception did not offer this possibility.

The medieval clerk was very much interested in man, viewed as a species, and a great deal of scholastic effort was directed to an exhaustive analysis of the subject. But this same clerk was not

47. Ibid., pp. 79–80.

particularly interested in individual men, even though he followed the actions of men in his chronicles with great interest.

The usual explanation of this paradox would be that medieval thought was too conceptual in nature, that it was too concerned with the generalization to pay very much attention to the particular instance. This explanation seems to me to propose a fallacious antithesis between the ability to observe particulars and the ability to generalize from them. It is a part of that hoary myth that modern science began when men, somehow and for some unexplained reason, went out and actually looked at nature.

As this chapter has shown, the medieval chronicler did not fail to observe the actors in his drama because he was too conceptual but because his concepts and categories of perception made it impossible to deal meaningfully with the individual. For the clerk, men were exactly like stones or planets—they might be exhaustively described by lists of attributes. There was no possibility of organizing or explaining such lists because their components were fundamentally unrelated. Thus it was inevitable that men as individuals should ordinarily be of no great interest; there was no way of dealing with them in a significant fashion.

This kind of perception greatly affected the way the clerk ordinarily lived his life. His categories of perception did not give him a means of judging consistency in conduct, and they did not give him a means for making that judgment about himself. From this limitation in his perceptual system arose the surprising inconsistencies in medieval life and thought. The very categories of perception of the medieval clerk presumed no ground for consistent human actions and inevitably made for a compartmentalization of experience.

CONCLUSION
The Middle Ages and Beyond

What we primarily mean by "medieval" is a kind of shape that experience assumed for men living at a particular time—or rather, we refer to one of two possible shapes to be found in the literature of the period. I would assume, although this study has not attempted to argue it, that many medieval artifacts besides those specifically considered in the text reflect these ways of seeing. Surely medieval art and architecture do.

For the clerk, meaningful experience assumed a kind of triadal shape; it presented itself as a preexistent norm, an intrusive interruption to that norm, and some sort of conclusion or readjustment. The active element in that shape, the interruption, was generated by attributes and not by objects, human or nonhuman. These attributes were necessarily attached to bodies, but they were not expressive of them. The experienced world of the clerk was a world of discrete and (at least ideally) self-contained actions arising in bodies, but separate from them.

The world of the clerk consequently differed from the modern world in two important respects. In the first place, it was nontemporal, as least as time is perceived today. Our modern feeling for time is a function of our feeling for process; time is the measure of continuous change. The discrete and self-contained character of action as perceived by the medieval clerk meant that the world could not be perceived as process. Secondly, the peculiar relationship between attributes and the objects in which they inhered meant that the objects—including human objects—were in the Middle Ages as unapproachable as prime matter.

The world of the aristocrat was unrelated to the world of the clerk. His was a world of values; experience was not to be investigated but to be appreciated. As a consequence, his perception of action was narrative in character. But this narrative was, by modern standards, thin, because it was not directed toward understanding. Furthermore, the public character of aristocratic values meant that good was ultimately to be located in one's posture. The aristocratic world of the Middle Ages was a universe of stances. As a consequence, it no more permitted the perception of human individuality, as it has been understood since the Renaissance, than did the clerical world.

These modes of perception are important for our understanding of individuals living at the time. If, for instance, the modern historian should seek to understand the behavior of Edward I or Stephen Langton, it would surely be wise to assume that they thought as other men of their time and station, and that medieval modes of perception both defined the way they perceived their world and limited their choice of actions. In exactly the same way, if Matthew Paris had an opportunity to write about Bismarck, he would have done well to rely heavily upon nineteenth- and twentieth-century estimates of his motives. The peril in writing about an age so different from our own is that we may modernize in the interest of charity—which is, of course, to assume some sort of ultimate validity for our own judgments.

On the other hand, these modes of perception as described are generalizations, which cannot, by the nature of things, prohibit exception. To ignore medieval modes of perception in evaluating a particular individual is one hazard, but another is to assume that when we have some clue about the mind of another period we can assert that every individual in that period was completely representative. If this were the case, men would still be thinking the thoughts of cave men. Men of exceptional vitality and intelligence can always think new thoughts. When two intellectual worlds exist simultaneously, as was the case in the Middle Ages, men may even learn to think in new ways, since each one may constitute, for the gifted individual, a criticism and correction of the other. John of Salisbury, Simon de Montfort, and Geoffrey Chaucer —these men bear an ambiguous relationship to their own time. Surely others did.

But a conclusion much more important emerges from this study. In the Middle Ages, modes of perception mediating experience were not innate; they were learned. Once learned, they were remarkably tenacious. They existed side by side for at least three hundred years (and probably much longer) without seriously modifying each other.

Furthermore, these modes of perception, viewed separately, were remarkably coherent. The clerk did not have one way of seeing nature and another way of perceiving men; both were perceived in the same way. And one is impressed, over and over, by the congruence with which action and objects were perceived. What I have called modes of perception in the Middle Ages were not different kinds of spectacles put on for one occasion or another. There was one pair of spectacles for all occasions. As a consequence, while the clerk and the aristocrat perceived experience differently, the experience of each was both coherent and self-consistent.

It appears that one can legitimately presume, at least for the purposes of investigation, that the relationship of modern man to his experience is no different. We too perceive experience by means of categories, and once learned, these categories become inclusive. This human situation, in its modern dress, seems to me to offer a most exciting challenge to the intellectual historian. He is in no better position than anyone else to speak of ultimate reality; he, too, approaches reality through the mediation of his perceptual categories. But there is at least the possibility that he can make conscious his a priori modes of perception. He cannot solve the problems, but he can, perhaps, move the discussion to a level at which real solutions may be possible. He can move the modern dialogues, between scientist and humanist, between the political left and right, and perhaps even between the different philosophical schools, to the presuppositions which at present inhibit communication.

Index